THE BASIS OF RACIAL
ADJUSTMENT

THE BASIS OF RACIAL ADJUSTMENT

BY

THOMAS JACKSON WOOFTER, JR.

Select Bibliographies Reprint Series

BOOKS FOR LIBRARIES PRESS
FREEPORT, NEW YORK

First Published 1925
Reprinted 1969

STANDARD BOOK NUMBER:
8369-5105-0

LIBRARY OF CONGRESS CATALOG CARD NUMBER:
75-99676

PRINTED IN THE UNITED STATES OF AMERICA

PREFACE

This book is primarily an effort to give the authentic facts concerning the different phases of Negro life in the United States today, with as little of the author's own bias as possible. The University Race Commission, composed of representatives of the Southern state universities deeply interested in race relations, has found that " there is a great need that the facts now available concerning the advancement of the Negro race in education, in professional accomplishment, in economic independence, and in character be studied by thoughtful students. This body of information would undoubtedly allay race antagonism and would serve as a foundation for tolerant attitude and intelligent action in every direction."

Thoughtful readers desiring to inform themselves on these matters have found it difficult, because there has been no one source to which they could go. This information has been so scattered that a disproportionate amount of time and effort has been necessary to get at the facts. In addition, many writers on the race question are so biased that they have unwittingly beclouded their facts with pages of special pleading or prejudice.

Any constructive program for the betterment of race relations must be firmly rooted in facts or it will inevitably fail. It must be based on a knowledge of the various phases of Negro life, of the effect of the Negro's presence on the various phases of community life, and of the constructive forces at work — the organizations and institutions which are successfully approaching the task of developing the Negro in harmony with American life and traditions. For this reason the material has been arranged so as to throw as much light as possible on the constructive activities and to help to answer the query What can we do to improve American life through better adjustment of our attitudes, our organizations, and our institutions to the Negro population, and what part can the Negro himself play in this adjustment?

The author has tried to avoid the expression " Negro problem." This is not a treatment of the Negro problem, but refers to the white man's problems as well as those of the Negro. The adaptations which the two races must make are mutual. But, as the first chapter indicates, race relations today present more tasks than problems, and these tasks of democratic racial action are also mutual. It is to the mutual interest of the white man and the colored man, the North and the South, that they be well performed. The white man's tasks are those of self-control in difficult situations and of adjusting American institutions so as to give the maximum service in aiding the belated race; the Negro's tasks are those of self-development, of cultivating family life, industry, thrift, and moral stamina.

Aside from the introductory chapters each chapter, after giving the background in some particular phase of Negro life, endeavors also to emphasize the most hopeful efforts to improve that phase. One force manifest in all these constructive efforts is the recent trend toward a more sympathetic and intelligent coöperation between the two races in working for their mutual advancement and for the progress of their common country.

THE AUTHOR

CONTENTS

vii

work Related.

isolate + compare the two.

→ use this as a neutral draw point.

THE BASIS OF
RACIAL ADJUSTMENT

CHAPTER I

MUTUAL SERVICE

There is now a much more substantial agreement on many of the so-called Negro problems than there has been in the past. Doctor Edgar Gardner Murphy, writing in 1904, said: "Because no ten men have ever yet agreed as to what we shall all do, the Negro presents something more than a task; he presents a problem." The lapse of twenty years has marked a genuinely encouraging tendency to dispel this disagreement. Not ten, but ten thousand men agree that the Negro must have equal justice in the courts, must receive training for life in the complex democracy of the United States, must be instructed and safeguarded in the preservation of health, and must receive a square deal in economic life. This substantial agreement is rapidly replacing the intellectual confusion which followed the Civil War.

RACIAL ADJUSTMENT A TASK

Prediction of the future status of the Negro may still be looked upon as a problem in guessing, but, for present situations, the Golden Rule offers a formula for constructive action which covers the ground as adequately to-day as it did two thousand years ago, and seemingly will continue to be effective in meeting future situations as they arise. Snap predictions of the future course of race relations have a habit of going astray. Whatever the future may hold, it is probable that the grandchildren and the great-grandchildren of the present generation will be far wiser in their time than their forebears; and in this wisdom they will be able to take care of themselves if they can only inherit a tradition of justice and sound ethics.

But individual agreement as to the justice of a policy does not immediately translate itself into community action. This is a process requiring material and moral resources. When it is agreed that the Negro needs schooling, there remains the task of supplying the funds, erecting the buildings, and manning them with competent teachers. Similarly when any ideal of racial adjustment is agreed upon, there remains the task of embodying the ideal into an effective program of community development. While the problematical features of the Negro's adjustment to life in American communities have diminished, the task of finding sufficient power and sufficient resources to accomplish the adjustment remains.

As doubts concerning the wisdom of constructive efforts have been dispelled, many more people have shown willingness to put their shoulders to the wheel of the vehicle of race relations whose heavy load has been brought over a road choked with obstacles. The tasks are being approached in a more determined spirit as more leaders volunteer for duty and as more resources are made available. This task of racial adjustment of white and Negro relationships is the greatest of all racial tasks in area, as well as in numbers involved. It is also the most intense, because the differences between white people and Negroes are greater than between any other American groups.

AMALGAMATION OR COÖPERATION?

It is often stated that when two races have lived side by side in the same area, under the same government, history has recorded only three results — extermination of the weaker, slavery, or amalgamation. Many people, therefore, think that only these three are possible. They believe that Booker Washington's ideal of the continuance of the white and colored races in the United States "as separate as the fingers, yet as united as the hand" is merely an impractical figure of speech. These people overlook the success of the Jews and Gypsies in maintaining racial integrity in many lands. No one affirms that the preservation of the racial integrity of the Jew is a denial of democratic principles. Democracy does not demand the fusion of races any more than it demands the fusion of religions.

Nor does history offer as a precedent any nation including two groups so numerous and so widely divergent in physical characteristics and position in the cultural scale as the white man and the Negro in the United States. Again, at no time recorded in history has such a wealth of spiritual and intellectual effort been directed toward the cultivation of satisfactory race relations as to-day. These conditions may make it possible for the ten million Negroes and the hundred odd million white people to dwell peacefully together without the tremendous social cost of amalgamation, each making its own peculiar contribution to the development of the United States.

INTERRACIAL MORALITY AND DEPENDENCE

Communities in which white and colored people live side by side need codes of race morals and programs of interracial action which will preserve American traditions and institutions, and, at the same time, allow a square deal to the colored people, and give them full opportunity to develop their capabilities and to contribute their share to the well-being and progress of the country. When communities permit prejudice or violence to prevent the law from protecting the life of the humblest citizen and from guaranteeing the integrity of the poorest home, they are as guilty as the individual who fails to control the passions which lead to the murder of a weaker neighbor. The taxation of colored people to pay a bond issue which is spent entirely for the erection of white public schools is just as dishonest in a community as the activity of the highwayman who, with the aid of a bludgeon, converts your cash to his own uses. These are the types of action to be avoided by interracial codes.

Aside from the dictates of morality, community self-interest demands a program of just and efficient interracial action. Experience has shown that in communities which neglect the legal protection of colored people, a class of white people is soon bred whose disrespect for the law passes beyond violence to colored people into acts which menace any weak citizen. By neglecting the education of colored people, lack of training is permitted to fasten the burdens of ignorance and inefficiency on all the people; by neglecting the living conditions and health of any of the citizens, disease zones are fostered which persistently menace the health of the whole community. To arrange community affairs so that these things will not occur because of the neglect of the Negro population is the challenging task of the hour for the rising generation.

COÖPERATION INCREASING

The most encouraging recent development in dealing with this task is to be found in rapid progress of the tendency to coöperate in working out interracial affairs, rather than to leave them to the outcome of bickering and struggle. The events of the Civil War and Reconstruction, with the inevitable wave of suffering, passion, and bitterness which flooded in their wake, virtually enthroned intolerance, and rendered coöperation between white and black and between North and South most difficult. But time, the great healer, has changed things so rapidly that intellectually honest persons can think together and, to an extent, work together for the improvement of many conditions affecting the two races.

There are still obdurate individuals, with more zeal than wisdom, who think that they alone could direct this great task of racial adjustment. In the North this phenomenon occurs in the man who can see nothing good in the South's dealings with the Negro, and who accepts any unverified rumor of wholesale slaughter of Negroes as typical of the attitude of all Southerners. In the South it occurs in the individual who thinks that it is not the "Yankee's" business to concern himself with colored people, and in the man whose dignity would never suffer him to consult with Negroes as to any policy. Among the Negroes, obduracy is manifested in a few who distrust white people in the aggregate and are suspicious of any advice or service, lest it contain a concealed degradation. But, fortunately, the relative influence of all three of these classes is waning before the growing power of coöperative groups which are successfully at work.

Many students of history get the impression that the relations between nations and races have been based largely on greed and conquest, and overlook the fact that the years between wars have been the fruitful seasons blessed by the development of the special abilities of many peoples to produce a variety of goods and services and exchange them peacefully with others, making bargains whereby both parties were benefited. Without such coöperation no division of highly specialized labor or of peculiarly valuable cultural and moral services would have been possible. The time of each nation or race would have been consumed with struggle to produce and keep the bare necessities. Thus through coöperation, the ethical and moral efforts of man have ever been more fruitful and more progressive than his rapacious conquests.

Full-flowered coöperation is a system wherein mutual aid is freely and spontaneously given because it is mutually beneficial. This coöperation is probably more perfectly illustrated in some of our humanized industrial plants than anywhere else. It is possible only through the exercise of intelligence, fairness, and the strictest morality; but even in its imperfect stages it enables men to divide and specialize the tasks of life so that not only is the effort to produce the necessities lessened, but the products are also improved. Men's minds are released from fear and their energies released from unnecessary competition and struggle, thereby creating a great surplus of time and energy which can be devoted to the adaptation of nature's soil, minerals, and climate to the comfort of man, and adaptation of man's own organizations and institutions to progress.

It is this latter road to full-fledged coöperation which is now open to the white people and the colored people of the United States. Their relationships have always been governed by principles of mutual aid in varying forms. Slavery has been tried and discarded by the white people themselves as inimical to their interests and inconsistent with their democracy. The paternalistic relationship, which characterized the plantation area until long after the Civil War, is passing as the large plantations fall into decay. As the Negro emerges from the plantation system and becomes an independent owner and renter of land and a city dweller with a measure of the white man's store of learning, he approaches the place where he can stand side by side with his white neighbor and work for the harmonious progress of the two races.

But there still remains the task of providing the ways and means for this coöperation and of enabling the Negro to live up to this opportunity to fit into American life. It is the greatest opportunity which has ever been presented to so large a number of colored people. It carries with it also a grave responsibility on the part of the Negro to meet it soberly and earnestly and to do his full share in harmonizing the interests of the masses of his race with those of the whole nation and in leading these masses away from ignorance and inefficiency.

The Nature of Racial Differences

Much has been written by biologists and anthropologists concerning the physical differences between the races. The question of whether these differences indicate a superiority of certain races and inferiority of others has been widely agitated. One school declares for a strict racial equality, at least a potential equality; while the other claims that racial differences are fixed and are transmitted from generation to generation, giving the possessor of superior qualities a perpetual superiority.

It might clarify the mind of a student torn between the claims of these two schools to realize that these scientists do not deal with the whole scale of human difference. Individuals may differ physically, mentally, culturally, or morally. The biologist is primarily interested in physical difference, secondarily in mental difference, and hardly interested at all in cultural and moral differences. But these cultural and spiritual factors are by far the most powerful in determining human situations; for, in organized society, it is more important to know how men will react to a common danger or a common opportunity than it is to know the angle of their faces or the thickness of their lips. The transmission of the cultural traits from generation to generation does not follow the laws of biological heredity at all. They are transmitted through social institutions. While the difference in the nasal index or head shape of two groups may be relatively fixed by heredity, the different reactions of an educated man and an ignorant man to a problem in compound interest or a public health situation may be equalized by education. This forces us to conclude that in dealing with human situations our ethics is of more use than our biology.

Even in regard to physical traits, however, biological research indicates that while individuals may differ widely, it is very difficult to classify rigidly the large groups of individuals which are known as races. It is difficult to find any trait or group of traits which separates them widely. Even skin color is a deceptive criterion, for there are black Jews and blond Indians. Within the white race there are varying degrees of blondness and among the African peoples there are wide varieties of blackness and brownness. Similarly when such traits as height, brain weight, keenness of vision or acuteness of hearing are measured, it is found that while the averages of the races differ slightly, the individual members of each race vary widely about the average. Thus while the average height of Japanese is low, the tallest Japanese are considerably taller than the shortest white men.

Even the physical criteria of race are not separate pigeon-holes into which individuals may be sorted and separated. They are slightly differing averages about which the individual members of the races vary so widely that there is much overlapping between the groups. This overlapping is due first to the fact that the essential equipment of humanity has always been much the same, and further to the fact that to-day there is no such thing as a pure race. Humanity differentiated into racial stocks in different isolated areas, but later wars, migrations, and voyages of discovery have brought about contacts and intermingling which have tended to equalize the original differences. The Tartar migrations and the infiltration of European business and missions into the Orient have mixed the white and yellow people. The contacts of Egypt and Phœnicia with Africa and the Arab migrations have made the so-called black race a varied group, and the hundreds of migrations and wars in Europe have caused a crossing and recrossing that have resulted in a highly complex stock.

It is also found that the differences in physical traits tend to change when races change their environment. Studies of the head form of immigrant children seem to indicate that the head form of the children tends to conform more closely to the average of the new environment than that of the parents.

Finally, in regard to physical and mental traits it is well to remember that even though the inheritance of the individual may be roughly fixed by biological heredity, this inheritance is so complex and includes so many possible combinations that the individual in a favorable environment has the power to make a good product out of a relatively poor inheritance, or, on the other hand, to deteriorate into a parasite in spite of a relatively rich inheritance.

The cultural differences between the world's peoples as they exist to-day are probably more marked than the physical and mental differences, but they are yielding more rapidly to the increasing ease of communication. In considering these differences the outstanding fact is that they are rooted in the common heritage of humanity, — a control over nature, and an ability for social organization. No one race was the exclusive inventor of its culture and hence none is its exclusive owner.

Written language, which is the greatest aid to social efficiency, originated with forgotten peoples, and the modern alphabet, which renders the language of the white man so efficient, is a gift from the Phœnicians; while the numerical system which is the basis of the highly developed mathematical system of the white man is a product of the Arab mind; and the origins of the wheel and the lever, those fundamental parts of modern mechanics, are lost in the dimness of the dawn of history.

To summarize : When the difference between men and the higher animals is considered, racial differences appear as slight differences in the average of human groups, about which individual members vary so widely that it is almost impossible to predicate a fixed criterion of race. Furthermore, these averages and the amount of variation change from time to time and place to place. The cultural differences, which form the truly important divisions of mankind, are not the exclusive heritage of any one race, and can, to a large degree, be equalized by the processes of education.

This evidence from the research of scientists is, therefore, not such as to warrant the assumption of an inborn, ineradicable superiority of one race over all others. Nevertheless it seems to be a human trait to assume such superiority. There are many peoples who arrogate it to themselves. That certain individuals are superior to others is undeniable, that certain groups contain a larger proportion of these superior individuals than others is probable, that certain peoples have been favored by environmental factors and cultural history is certain. But to assume that every member of an advantaged group is superior to every member of a disadvantaged group is a blind error, and the assumption that group differences are fixed and ineradicable for all time is equally as mistaken. It is desirable frankly to recognize the differences as they actually exist, but there is absolutely no ethical justification for the assumption that an advantaged group has an inherent right to exploit and oppress, and the prejudice based upon such assumptions is the most vicious enemy to human peace and coöperation.

The ethical attitude to assume toward the relation of races is, therefore, one which recognizes the worth and merit of individual personalities wherever they are found, and which fosters the development of a social system which will give all peoples the chance to assimilate the common culture of humanity and coöperate for the common progress of mankind.

Racial Differences Help Specialization

Fortunately racial differences are no bar to coöperation, but rather, when they are useful differences, they are actually helpful. If all men were exactly alike, specialization would not be so effective as it is when special abilities can be developed and put to work for special ends. To argue, therefore, that the Negro and the white man are very different, is a point in favor of, rather than against, their coöperation. As long as their fundamental interests in a prosperous and progressive democracy are the same, their useful differences will enable them to render valuable mutual aid.

Fifty years of freedom have not been nearly sufficient to discover just what the special aptitudes of the Negro are. There is reason to suppose, however, that he has ability to contribute to American life in music, art, and probably in the drama. His folk music is in a class by itself. Some of its pathos and some of its jazz have gained currency in American tunes. The pictures of Tanner, the stories made famous by Uncle Remus, the poetry of Dunbar, the essays of Fisher, the perfect buffoonery of Bert Williams, the powerful emotional acting of Gilpin, and the songs of Roland Hayes, are all indicative of the promise of the future.

It may be, also, that from his long and absorbing contact with natural forces, the Negro will have his own peculiar contribution to make to the development of the natural sciences. Benjamin Banneker, an astronomer of note, is credited with having fashioned one of the first clocks made in America. George W. Carver to-day has gained international reputation for his peculiar genius in the chemical analysis of the homely things close at hand, and their adaptation to useful purposes. From the peanut, potato, pecan, and native clays of Alabama, he has produced a bewildering series of more than three hundred products. It is certain that the colored man has some special contribution to make to American life if he only bestirs himself to develop his own peculiar strong points and is aided by the white man to develop these capabilities and find places where they fit into the scheme of American progress.

MUTUAL ACQUAINTANCE

The essentials of effective coöperation between the races are mutual acquaintance, mutual confidence, and mutual interests. Even in the South where the races are in closest contact, mutual acquaintance, or the possession by each race of knowledge as to the real facts concerning the other, is by no means widespread. Notwithstanding the assertion so often made in the South that "We know all about the Negro," it is safe to venture that only a very small proportion of the white people know the general, present-day conditions well. Tradition and prejudice, the ancient enemies of scientific knowledge, operate so powerfully in race questions that the facts are often obscured. The slaveholders of the old South knew the Negroes well because they were in intimate contact with them, and because Negroes were, in those days, a comparatively simple group, almost totally illiterate, bound to the soil, and tutored by the owners themselves. To-day the ex-slaveholder, or the slaveholder's son, knows the tradition as to what the Negro was sixty years ago, which is vastly different from what the Negro is to-day. Or perchance, if he farms with Negro labor, he knows the Negro farm hand of to-day, who is a vastly different man from the city dweller. The great class of Negro leaders, — business men, teachers, preachers, and doctors, — are altogether out of touch with the white people. Nine out of ten white men do not number a single one of these among their personal acquaintances.

To quote from Dr. Edgar Gardner Murphy's "The Present South":

We may be tempted to say, therefore, that the kindlier conception of the old-time Negro resulted from the fact that the white world at its best was looking upon the Negro at his best; the harsher conception of the present Negro resulting from the fact that a white world which is not its best is looking upon the Negro at his worst.

The first task of coöperation is, therefore, the cultivation of a mutual acquaintance based upon accurate knowledge. Each race needs to give more sober thought to the other and needs painstakingly to separate facts from dogma and demagoguery. This is a process of study and the cultivation of friendly contacts. It is impossible to overstate the need for real facts as a basis for action.

One thing which is essential to the appreciation of the facts concerning race relations is the dynamic viewpoint. A sense of the value of the time element is necessary. The civic and economic status of the Negro to-day is vastly different from what it was fifty years ago. As the civic and economic life of the race changes, race relations change.

No one can afford to dogmatize as to the present on the basis of the facts of the past. No one can afford to predict the future without a very thorough knowledge of the present-day trends.

In addition to the dynamic viewpoint the constructive viewpoint is essential. The programs which stimulate progress must be based upon the constructive forces at work. It is necessary to know the organizations and institutions which are successfully approaching the task of improving race relations and the principles upon which their success is based. Such a dynamic and constructive analysis of the facts is fundamental to the mutual acquaintance which coöperation demands.

This kind of knowledge is most essential for the rising generation of colored people to-day, for it is the usual experience of belated races that, when they begin to rise in the scale of knowledge and begin to comprehend the extent of their backwardness, they are engulfed in self-pity, which may embitter or may greatly discourage them. Public opinion among colored people in the United States is to-day in this critical stage. Sometimes the Negro ascribes to prejudice conditions which arise, at least partially, from his own backwardness. This tendency is seen in the discontent with the tenant system which is as much the result of the ignorance and improvidence of farm labor as it is of abuses by unscrupulous landlords. The Negro also sometimes blames racial injustice for conditions which are common to all races and classes occupying a similar economic or social status. Much of the hardship imposed on the Negro in court proceedings is shared by the friendless, moneyless white man. In other words, a proper perspective on the facts shows that many of the difficulties of the Negro are not racial but are inherent in the economic, political, and judicial systems of the United States or in the condition of the Negro, and can improve only as these improve.

This is a process which takes time. Social progress is not the product of sudden changes but of a multitude of gradual improvements with an occasional revolutionary reorganization. It is therefore especially important for Negroes in their present state of mind to appreciate fully the time element in racial adjustment. The impartial student of the facts of Negro life in America will find much that is genuinely encouraging and practically nothing to warrant a feeling of hopelessness. Analysis of the successful constructive movements will show that in the interest of getting results the colored people should guard against self-pity and undue impatience.

Mutual Confidence

Mutual confidence can come only after fear and jealousy, which is a corollary of fear, have been dispelled. The most fallacious of fears arise from the feeling that what is the Negro's gain must of necessity be the white man's loss. As a matter of fact there is ample opportunity in America for both. Many are the out-worn fears of the past concerning the Negro. Former discussions of Negro education involved fears that it would lead to vanity in life; that it would spoil a good field hand by teaching books; and some even went so far as to predict that learning would only make the Negro an arch criminal. Those who are familiar with the records of the thousands of Negro graduates who are proving their worth to-day know the absurdity of these past fears. Of course, few of these graduates go back to work on the farm for twenty dollars a month, but their good influence as community leaders reflects back upon those who do remain. It would be almost impossible to find one whose efficiency has not been increased by training, and it is relatively rare that a trained Negro is accused of crime.

Such groundless fears as these must go, for as long as there is fear there will be distrust and stifling oppression. The mutual confidence which must replace fear is to be based on the knowledge that each race is genuinely and sympathetically interested in the other, and that both are deeply concerned with the progress of their common country. This mutual confidence cannot be conjured from the air by thought or will power. It comes through experience and can be cultivated by beginning to work together in a sympathetic and earnest spirit. In this respect the best way to learn coöperation is to begin to coöperate on simple, everyday matters.

MUTUAL INTERESTS

The mutual interests essential to coöperation between white and black in the United States are so obvious that they need not be dwelt upon. The two races living side by side are so intimately connected that it is difficult to find a point at which one may be affected without also affecting the other. All community activities — government, farming, business, education, religion, health, and humane care of the unfortunates — are complicated by reason of the presence of two races, both of which need the same kind of community work. Thus the tasks of racial adjustment cross-section the tasks of democracy. The maximum advancement for either race is conditioned by the advancement of the other. Their mutual interests are too vital to be left to debate and conflict. They are big enough to deserve approach in the great spirit of mutual aid.

BIBLIOGRAPHY [1]

BOAZ, FRANZ. The Mind of Primitive Man, Chapters IX and X.

BRYCE, JAMES. Relations of the Advanced to the Backward Races of Mankind. Romanes Lectures, 1902.

Handbook of Interracial Coöperation. Commission on Interracial Coöperation, Atlanta, Georgia.

MURPHY, E. G. The Present South, pp. 160–171.

OLDHAM, J. H. Christianity and the Race Problem, Chapters IV, V, and VI.

WASHINGTON, B. T. Address before the Atlanta Exposition — Up from Slavery, Chapter XIV; The Story of the Negro, Chapter XV.

WEATHERFORD, W. D. The Negro from Africa to America, Chapter XV.

WHITE and JACKSON. Poetry by American Negroes.

TOPICS FOR STUDY AND DISCUSSION

1. Compare the relative importance, in the United States, of the following groups, considering in each case relative numbers and cultural differences: Indians, Mongolians, Mexicans, other foreign born, Negroes. Make this comparison for a single state.

2. How do racial differences aid in the division of labor and the distribution of social burdens?

[1] These bibliographies at the end of each chapter are suggestive rather than exhaustive. No periodical matter is included, and, as much valuable material has appeared in magazines, the reader who desires to go exhaustively into a subject should consult the Periodical Guides. The aim has been to include the most suggestive reading for beginners, confining the references as far as possible to books which should be available in average college and city libraries. Two books not specifically mentioned but which are valuable as references for statistics on all topics are the Negro Year Book, published annually by Tuskegee Institute, and a special report of the United States Census Bureau entitled Negro Population in the United States, 1790–1915. The latter will, of course, have to be supplemented by reference to the 1920 census. An exhaustive bibliography is given in the Negro Year Book.

3. In what sense are the tasks of adjusting race relations "white man's problems" rather than "Negro problems"?

4. Study an anthology of Negro verse ("Poetry by American Negroes," White and Jackson), a collection of folk songs ("Folk Songs and Folklore of the American Negro," Odum), and the folk tales of Uncle Remus, and comment on the possibility of special contributions by Negroes to American culture.

5. Compile from the Negro Year Book a list of Negro inventors and inventions.

6. The historical background of race relations in the United States has centered around the slave trade, the extension of slavery, the abolition of slavery, and the adjustment of freedmen to democratic institutions. Has this been a background which would produce a rational attitude or an attitude based on controversy?

7. Outline the mutual interests of white people and Negroes in the United States.

8. Some people say that the best way to treat a race problem is to leave it alone. If this policy is followed by the wise and unselfish people, are there other classes who will not leave it alone? What will be the effect?

9. Has science demonstrated the inherent superiority or inferiority of any one race?

CHAPTER II

LEADING TO RACIAL COÖPERATION

Race relations are entering a new phase, as different from any past phase as freedom was from slavery. The most potent factor in the situation is the rising group of young leaders of both races. The Negro is emerging from the tutelage of the white man and relying more and more on the advice and effort of his own leaders. Slavery was a school where the Negro learned under the direct tutelage of the white man. It was a hard school, but it taught him the fundamental lessons of work, thrift, and religion, and he learned them reasonably well. Reconstruction and the decades immediately following saw the Negro again completely under white leadership. In this period, which has not yet passed from some backward communities, many of his leaders exploited him economically and politically. But while unscrupulous planters and carpet-bag politicians were exploiting him, another group of white people was building and teaching schools, thereby laying the foundation for the new era in colored leadership, and hundreds of ex-slaveholders were aiding former slaves to purchase lands or small businesses, thereby laying the foundation for the economic prosperity of the present generation. Much progress was made in these years, but it was made under the guidance of the white man.

NEW NEGRO LEADERSHIP

With the first decades of the twentieth century the new era commences. Every Southern state has built for Negroes a public school system, manned by Negro teachers and supervised by white state, county, and city boards of education. During the past school year some fourteen million dollars were spent from public funds for teachers' salaries in these schools. The genius of Booker T. Washington has built at Tuskegee an educational institution unique in its adaptation to the training of a belated people. He has furnished a philosophy of interracial coöperation and stimulated in the Negro a racial pride which is replacing the blind desire to imitate the white man. The denominations have built colleges for training leaders. A separate Negro press has developed more than four hundred weekly and monthly papers. The few ex-slaves who purchased land have been succeeded by over two hundred thousand farm owners and an equal number of renters operating more than twenty million acres of land. The small businesses have grown to fifty thousand in number, with an annual income of over a billion dollars. From dependency for religious instruction upon seats in the gallery of white churches, the Negro has developed a reliance upon large denominations of his own, with twenty thousand preachers, organized mission boards, and a system of denominational schools. Doctors, nurses, dentists, and lawyers have rapidly formed a colored professional group.

With this development, the Negro has passed, to a large degree, under the leadership of his own race. It is natural that there should be a diversity of leadership, because the colored group has become greatly diversified. Seventy years ago the population, with the exception of a few skilled tradesmen and domestic servants, was entirely confined to farming in the rural South. A third of the colored people now live in cities and a fifth are in the North. They traverse the whole range of American life as farmers, teachers, preachers, doctors, skilled tradesmen, merchants, editors, bankers, and small-scale manufacturers. It is almost impossible to realize the deep significance of such fundamental changes effected in such a short space of time. The leadership which the situation demands is important in the extreme.

STRATEGIC IMPORTANCE OF LEADERS

The colored leader is the keystone of the arch of race relations to-day. Upon his shoulders, in large degree, rests the responsibility not only for the well-being of his own group, but also for the peace and progress of large areas of the United States. A race or nation which has to be continually looked after, a race for which some one else has to do the thinking, will never progress. It is only through the development of its own leadership that the Negro race can serve itself, — can exert its own efforts to progress, and can learn those lessons which are taught only in the strict school of experience.

If the race leader is wise and coöperative, working for such advances among his people as are harmonious with the development of the whole country, then he has a real contribution to make to the history of the United States, and indirectly to the history of race relations throughout the world. For other nations, especially those with black

colonies, are beginning to turn to the United States to find
out how the progress of our colored people has been attained
with so little friction. On the other hand, if the colored
leader is unwise, placing the advantage of the moment or
selfish interests ahead of the long-time advantage, and advocating non-coöperation and agitation to gain his ends, then
the bickering, unrest, litigation, and violence which arise
from such a policy will inevitably impede the progress of
racial coöperation.

The effectiveness of coöperation rather than agitation
when real results are desired, stands out in the following
narrative:

A young state farm demonstration agent was planning to
hold a county-wide meeting of colored farmers for the purpose of preparing them to cope with the boll weevil and to
improve their farming generally. Several outstanding white
leaders favored his work and arranged for the meeting to be
held in the county courthouse. Other leaders, who did not
realize the importance of this work and who were faction-
ally opposed to the backers of the movement, began to agi-
tate against the use of the courthouse by Negroes. As some
of them expressed it, Negroes should use the courthouse
in that county only as defendants. The opposition worked
on prejudice to such an extent that feeling ran rather high
and the community was split into two factions. About two
weeks before the meeting was to be held the colored demonstration agent was waited on by the opposition and forced
to leave town. Had he been an unwise leader, giving inflammatory interviews to the papers and making fire-eating
speeches to his people, he might have attracted marked
attention to himself and very unfavorable comment upon

that county. One of the editors of a near-by city daily wanted to write a scathing article about the incident but the Negro was too wise. He asked this editor to ignore the incident and write an article praising his meeting, and commending the town for allowing it to be held in the courthouse. The next step of the demonstration agent was to go to a prominent editor of another city daily which was circulated widely in the county, and secure his consent to speak at the meeting, with a published announcement of his decision. The colored demonstrator then got the mayor of the county seat in which the meeting was to be held to appoint an entertainment committee for their prominent editor guest, and on this committee were placed the leaders of the opposition. They were informed that the out-of-town guest ought not to know of the split in the community but should be entertained with a hospitality which his prominence merited.

So the day of the meeting dawned with the opposition silenced and a great crowd of country people, white and black, on hand to hear the speaking. Of course, when the program was outlined, when the farmers were urged to diversify their crops, to raise their own foodstuffs, to improve their homes, and to encourage their children by getting them into corn clubs, pig clubs, and canning clubs, even those who had been opposed to the meeting began to see the benefits. The out-of-town editor made a sweeping speech, congratulating the men of the county for their coöperative spirit. The colored demonstrator accomplished his objective without making enemies, without embittering his own people, and without calling attention to an unfortunate situation which to begin with was more a small-town factional squabble than a racial matter.

A short time later the government funds ran low and this demonstrator communicated with his clubs, telling them that he would not be able to visit them as often as formerly on account of the lack of adequate traveling expenses. They pooled their resources to buy him a car and two of the men who had been among the most strenuous opponents of his courthouse meeting contributed the largest amounts toward the purchase and are now the most cordial friends of his work. He gained his objective by matching bitterness with diplomacy and prejudice with a demonstration of worth.

Radical and Coöperative Leaders

With the rise of a special Negro leadership there is a danger that the new leaders, in their eagerness to press the immediate, special needs of their people, will lose sight of the fact that the interests of the ten million colored people in the United States are, in the long run, inextricably bound up with those of the hundred million white people. This seems already to be the case with a certain cult of Negro leaders, most of whom are editors and politicians.

There are two distinct schools of colored leaders, one advocating hard work and gradual advance, the other insistent in its demands for equality, and constantly agitating and litigating for the immediate realization of its desires. The former is composed mainly of Southern teachers, preachers, and business men who are working among the masses of their own people. The latter comprises, for the most part, Northern editors and politicians.

When the desires of these two schools of leaders are compared there is very little substantial difference. Both want the following things:

1. Immediate cessation of interracial violence, especially lynching.

2. Better educational facilities and just distribution of public school funds.

3. Equality of economic opportunity — equal pay for the same work, opportunity to advance in the scale as ability is demonstrated, and such impartial enforcement of laws as will protect them from exploitation.

4. Better living conditions, especially in paving, lighting, sanitation, and police protection in Negro neighborhoods.

The sharp differences arise over politics and "social equality." The school of Southern Negro leaders knows that Southern white people, particularly those in counties where the colored population is in the majority, are not yet willing to countenance a second experiment in turning the reins of government over to the mass of colored people without any restriction. The bitter experiences of reconstruction are too fresh in their minds and pressure only tends to cement their determination on this point. As it is, however, there are increasing numbers who qualify and vote in the South. Some three thousand are registered in Atlanta, and their votes help decide such issues as bond elections and charter amendments. In Kentucky, Tennessee, and in parts of Virginia and North Carolina their suffrage is unrestricted. The white primary, of course, excludes them from choice of Democratic candidates, and the choice of these candidates is equivalent to election to office.

That vague term "social equality" includes anything from intermarriage to riding in the same railway coach. From a scientific viewpoint, anthropologists have been unable to agree on the physical results of race mixture, but the sociologists agree that the social cost of the mixture of heterogeneous types is prohibitive. But this is a problem which will be taken care of by individual taste. To ninety-nine out of a hundred white people, and to a growing number of colored people, intermarriage is unthinkable, and relegated to the background. As for the "Jim Crow" ordinances, the agitating school want them abolished immediately, while the others endure them because they are the fiat of the ruling class. Still others feel that the Negro is really happier by himself, provided he receives equal accommodations for equal pay. They feel further that, as a matter of policy, in places where the mass of Negroes would come in contact with white people, much friction is averted by these customs.

Although the platforms of these two factions are similar, their methods are very different, especially in respect to the time in which they hope to accomplish results. To any one who is thoroughly familiar with the backward condition of the Negro, the impatience of some of his leaders seems inevitable. On the other hand, the progress which he has been able to make in education, business, farming, and home ownership, despite these handicaps, has been phenomenal. It has not been equaled by any large group of black people anywhere else in the world.

Between the two types of Negro leaders there is also a great psychological gulf. One believes in earning rights. The other feels that rights are inherent and believes in demanding them. The effect upon others of demanding rights is vastly different from that of earning them. The demand often antagonizes the man whose good will is necessary, while quiet worthiness is inevitably recognized. The wisest leaders of minority groups the world over have always pursued the conciliatory course.

There will probably always be these two classes of Negro leaders, as there is usually a radical and a conservative wing of every cult. This is especially true since there is a large and growing Negro population in the North, where their community problems and relations to white people are quite different from those in the South. When the results obtained are measured, however, the score is easily in favor of the coöperative worker. This is true because the active aid of the average American can be enlisted much more readily by a demonstration than by a bludgeon. In fact the agitating type of leader is rarely seen among the masses of his people in the South and never heard by Southern people, while leaders of the type of Doctor R. R. Moton draw large audiences and are favorably received even in the heart of the Black Belt.

What Leadership Demands

In almost every instance Negro leaders, whatever may be their philosophy of race relations, are self-made men. There is no third generation of riches and education in the group. Booker Washington and his successor, Robert R. Moton, were born in slavery, as was George W. Carver, the black wizard of chemistry, and many lesser local leaders still living. The others are either sons of slaves or of parents freed shortly before the Civil War. A realization of this lowly origin and struggle for education and position will aid in appreciating the weak and the strong points of these men. They have all the faults and all the virtues of other self-made men. Poise, unselfishness, broader vision of life, and adherence to standards are the traits which the training of future leaders should emphasize.

Poise is difficult for a Negro leader of to-day, because of the delicacy of his position and the impatience of his following. It is easy for the agitator to lose patience completely and become too much of a "reformer" or too much of a nuisance. On the other hand, the coöperative leader must watch his position carefully lest his white friends think he is trying to go too fast or his colored enemies attack him for going too slowly. With the amount of jealousy which exists between the leaders, even a fancied ground for criticism is often enough to bring on an avalanche of vituperation.

Selfishness is not predominant among Negro leaders, but self-advertisement becomes an obsession with some, especially if they are in positions where they are compelled to raise money for their cause. In these cases their agitation and publicity are designed to attract attention to themselves rather than to forward the interests of their race. Occasionally there arises one who is wholly selfish, for whom the weakness and gullibility of the mass of colored people is too great a temptation. These demagogues are usually orators, skilled at playing upon the ills of their people. Like the patent medicine fakir who describes symptoms until every one in the audience is in fear of death and is willing to pay for any remedy that may be handed out, they describe injustices until all their hearers feel aggrieved and are willing to join or subscribe to anything that offers a remote possibility of aid. One leader of this type has just been convicted by a United States court, after having collected several million dollars from his deluded victims and having almost caused international complications by his violent agitation against white nations, especially colonial nations. Many of the Negro politicians have imitated their white colleagues by adopting these tactics.

Broader vision of life and adherence to higher standards are both products of training in its fullest sense, not only that training which comes in schools, but also that which comes from ripe experience. It was noted in the beginning that a new generation of Negro college graduates is assuming the reins. It must not be thought, however, that these are all as fully trained as white college graduates. The majority of their schools are still weak in teaching force and equipment and almost wholly lacking in the specialization necessary for leadership in the professions.

The medical profession illustrates this perfectly. There are only two colored medical schools. Of the graduates of these two schools very few have the requisite hospital experience for a superior rating. In other lines the deficiency in training facilities is as marked. The average colored teacher has considerably less than a full grammar school training and very little special training for teaching. The output of the normal schools is not nearly sufficient to supply the new teachers needed each year. For recruiting a body of twenty thousand ministers the output of theological schools is only about two hundred and fifty a year, and the courses in these schools are rather narrow. The future Negro leadership is therefore hampered by the tardy development of these training facilities.

RESPONSIBILITY OF WHITE LEADERS

The progress of the colored population in harmony with the progress of the nation brings leadership responsibilities to the white people also. The advice and guidance which colored leaders need, the aid in developing facilities for training real leaders, and the philanthropy needed for building institutions, must come largely from white men. The white man must extend a helping and a guiding hand to assist the colored man to his goal of progress in harmony with American life. Negroes generally recognize their dependence in this respect upon the members of the majority race. But the substitution of the present Negro leadership for the tutelage of the white slave owner has caused a natural chasm between the outstanding members of the two races. As the Negro was released from slavery, the more able and energetic members of the race entered business and the professions serving their own people, thus cutting themselves off from the intimate view of the white people. As they rose in the scale of progress they passed above the observation of white fellow citizens. This left the two races in the position of two pyramids, in contact at the base but widely separated at the peak.

INTERRACIAL COMMITTEES

Realization of this situation led, in 1919, to the organization of the Commission on Interracial Coöperation, a movement of Southern white and colored people, which has spread through 800 Southern counties. This movement is primarily an effort to bring the leaders of the two races back into contact, — to enable them to coöperate in community affairs.

The inaugurators of this movement recognized the mutual dependence of the two races and knew that, in any community, efficiency depends upon the education of all the people ;

that violence, whether toward white or black men, endangers all law; that health can be attained only by attacking disease wherever it shows itself; and that bad moral conditions are a menace to the community, whether they are in the colored or in the white neighborhood. They also recognize that the correction of these conditions is a task great enough to demand a combination of the best efforts of both races. County and state interracial committees are endeavoring to supply this harmonious combination of leadership for good work in the community.

The fact that these committees are organized by counties is one of the strong points of the movement, for the county committee is on the ground to deal intimately with local situations; and after all, the great tasks of adjusting race relations are nothing more than the sum total of the tasks involved in numbers of local communities. Each community has its slightly variant local situation to meet and each, to an extent, is human in that it would prefer to deal with its own affairs rather than be lectured to by an outside agency. This attitude applies especially to questions of race relations, because accusations and counter-accusations in the past have been so acrimonious that there has grown up in each community a tender sensitiveness, a psychology of self-defense which often leads to the misunderstanding of well-meaning efforts of outsiders to aid. Thus the Commission on Interracial Coöperation has recognized the strategic importance of the local leaders who are on the job in a great number of places. These, rather than the general national personalities, are the primary factors in racial adjustment.

The significance of local effort is emphasized in the December 1923 message of President Coolidge: "But it is well to recognize that these difficulties are to a large extent local problems which must be worked out by the mutual forbearance and human kindness of each community. Such a method gives much more promise of a real remedy than outside interference."

The Commission is a southwide body meeting once a year and dealing with national organizations and movements relating to colored people. Through contacts with editors it has been useful in molding public opinion and it is building a literature of coöperation; through work in colleges it has promoted study and research; through contacts with denominational boards it has quickened the interest of the churches; and through special women's work it has reached numbers of women's organizations with a constructive program.

The concrete situations are, however, attacked by the state and local committees. State committees of South Carolina and Georgia have coöperated with Methodist Home Mission societies in placing Negro nurses in the state departments of health, and state committees in Tennessee and South Carolina have aided in the establishment of girls' reform schools. The Georgia State Committee is interested in a similar project. In Tennessee such a sentiment was worked up that members of the white women's clubs appeared before the legislature in behalf of the bill. State legislators have been approached regarding increased appropriations for Negro institutions, and state railroad commissions influenced to work for better accommodations for Negro passengers. Legal aid work has been fostered by several committees.

The following specific accomplishments of local committees illustrate their value to their communities:

ATLANTA, GEORGIA. Securing a million and a quarter of bond money for colored schools; securing park from city and county; coöperation in adjustment of Negroes to community chest; coöperation in opening new day nursery.

AUGUSTA, GEORGIA. Participation in community survey out of which grew legal aid work.

SAVANNAH, GEORGIA. Securing girls' detention home, tuberculosis and children's clinic, day nursery, and improvement at hospital.

CHATTANOOGA, TENNESSEE. Improvement of living conditions. Addition of library to high school.

DAYTONA, FLORIDA. Community nurse.

NASHVILLE, TENNESSEE. Coöperation in establishing legal aid bureau.

NEW ORLEANS, LOUISIANA. Coöperation with local civic league.

LOUISVILLE, KENTUCKY. Coöperation with community chest, alleviation of friction growing out of political campaign.

In numbers of places violence has been averted by prompt action of these committees in a crisis, and in numbers of places committees have kept the needs of the Negro schools before the boards of education until they have been improved.

This partial list gives an idea of the diversity of community needs which these committees meet. In fact each committee is left to fix its own program in accordance with the most pressing local needs as they are outlined by the colored leaders.

The meetings of these committees provide a forum, a platform from which the races can speak soberly and sympathetically with each other. It is bad for any community that there should be two distinct classes, each ignorant of the thoughts and purposes of the other. Under these circumstances slight but very irritating grievances often arise through thoughtlessness, grievances which could have been removed instantly had they been made known.

While these committees are in position to accomplish good, concrete results for the community, their by-product in good will is fully as valuable as their principal product in good works. The mere meeting together for common benefit lays the foundation for still more effective coöperation. It generates mutual confidence and creates a sphere of good will which harmonizes the lives of the two races as nothing else could possibly do.

In the words of the prominent Negro author and editor, Isaac Fisher,

It (the Commission) has already provided points of contact between the better classes of the two races in many places; it has already set sentinels of both races to watch for signs of disorder and causes of friction; it has already taken the lead, again and again, as our records show, in preventing violence in certain places; it has repeatedly called the attention of officials to unfair attitudes toward Negroes in several places, and with successful results; without publicity, it is courageously serving notice on souls here and there, who do not have the vision of good will and fair play, that the voices of Christian white people will not be silent any longer where inequitable practices obtain. It has not revolutionized racial conditions here, but it has established the basis of race adjustment by providing for the coöperation and good will which spring out of perfect understanding. There is quite a long distance to go yet; but we are certainly headed in the right direction.

This responsibility for coöperative leadership is not entirely confined to the South. In resorting to arms to settle the issues of the Civil War the nation assumed responsibility for the Negro. Emancipation destroyed a great part of the wealth of the South and left the Negro on the hands of an impoverished section. The national government soon withdrew its aid and thus the South was left alone with its problems. In this situation Northern philanthropy came to the rescue and has played a leading part in the establishment of colored colleges, high schools, and industrial schools. The time has not yet come for the withdrawal of this interest in the tasks which belong largely to all sections of the nation.

BIBLIOGRAPHY

BRAWLEY, BENJ. A Short History of the American Negro, Chapter XV.

DuBois, W. E. B. The Souls of Black Folk.

HART, A. B. The Southern South, Chapter XXVII.

HASKIN, ESTELLE. Handicapped Winners.

HAYNES, ELIZABETH. Unsung Heroes.

HAYNES, GEORGE. The Trend of the Races, pp. 14–17; 69–79; 91–98.

KERLIN, R. T. The Voice of the Negro, Introduction, Chapters I and II.

Literature of Commission on Interracial Coöperation.

MOTON, R. R. Finding a Way Out.

MURPHY, E. G. The Present South, pp. 171–176.

Bulletins Nos. 38–39 of the United States Bureau of Education, 1916. "Negro Education in the United States," pp. 3–7.

PHILLIPS, U. B. Plantation and Frontier Documents, Introduction.

WASHINGTON, B. T. and DuBois, W. E. B. The Negro in the South.

WEATHERFORD, W. D. The Negro from Africa to America, Chapter XVI.

TOPICS FOR STUDY AND DISCUSSION

1. Consult Negro Year Book for items showing Negro progress in the past fifty years. Note signs of progress in a particular community.

2. Study Negro periodicals (*Chicago Defender, The Negro World, The Crisis, The Messenger, Atlanta Independent, Oklahoma Black Dispatch, New York Age,* etc.) and see Kerlin,

"The Voice of the Negro," for signs of radicalism, impatience, and bitterness, or coöperation among Negro leaders.

3. Consult Census, Negro Year Book, and Negro Education in the United States for estimate as to the number and training of the leadership classes.

4. What is the relative value of a movement or institution for Negroes directed by white people and a movement or institution for Negroes directed by Negroes? What are the advantages of mixed directorates? Answer on the basis of the work of an organization which you can observe.

5. If there is an interracial committee in a community with which you are familiar, study its origin and development and the factors which make for its success or failure.

6. What general effect have political leaders had on race adjustment?

7. What classes of the two races are in closest contact? From the characteristics of these classes would you say that these contacts are helpful or harmful?

8. What local situations could be best handled by interracial committees? (See literature of Commission on Interracial Coöperation.)

9. Is the Negro's natural disposition patient and kindly or impatient and bitter? What is responsible for the growing tendency in the latter direction? How can it be remedied?

10. Discuss the characteristics of the two types of Negro leaders.

CHAPTER III

GROWTH AND DISTRIBUTION OF NEGRO POPULATION

The growth and spread of the Negroes in the United States is in itself a phenomenon in social physics which is almost unprecedented. Beginning three hundred years ago with the handful of Africans who were landed at Jamestown, the population has increased to ten and a half million. Historians estimate that at most only about 350,000 Africans were brought to this country as slaves before 1808; yet some five million were emancipated by the Civil War. The difference between this number and the 350,000 imported shows how the Negro race thrived even in slavery, their natural increase in two hundred years amounting to four and a half million. The sixty years of freedom have brought another increase of over five million, bringing the total in 1920 to 10,463,000. Aside from native-born white men, they constitute the largest group in the United States and include about a tenth of the total population of the country.

RATE OF INCREASE

At different times two extreme opinions have been held as to the rate of increase of the Negro population. For a while alarmists pointed to the great fecundity of the .

colored people, and predicted that within a short time the country would be overrun with Negroes. In 1883 E. G. Gilliam estimated that by 1980 there would be 200,000,000 Negroes in the United States. A short time after the abolition of slavery, however, the operation of the more normal forces which tend toward equilibrium in the population threw confusion into the ranks of these prophets by sharply slackening the rate of Negro increase. The pendulum of conjecture then swung to the other extreme. Predictions were freely made that the Negro was dying out and would shortly become a vanishing factor in the life of the nation.

The facts, however, do not bear out either of these extreme views. Indeed, the forces acting upon the Negro population are so varied and the resultant changes so rapid that predictions are very unsafe. The census figures do show, however, that the colored population is not increasing as rapidly as it did in the past. From 1870 to 1880 the increase was 22 per cent; from 1880 to 1890, 18 per cent; from 1890 to 1900, 14 per cent; from 1900 to 1910, 11 per cent; and from 1910 to 1920, 6 per cent. Thus the complexities of freedom have brought a people which originally had all the fecundity of a tropical race to the point where their increase is almost as sluggish as that of the French, whose birth and death rates barely balance.

After the Census of 1900, Wilcox, a very careful estimator, figured that if the tendencies between 1870 and 1900 continued to operate, the Negro population in the year 2000 would not be greater than twenty-five million. He predicted the following approximate rates between 1900 and 2000:

Period	Per Cent Increase in Negro Population
1900–1920	30.2
1920–1940	26.2
1940–1960	22.2
1960–1980	18.2
1980–2000	14.2

The censuses of 1910 and 1920, however, fell so far short of this estimate that Wilcox has recently revised his prediction downward. Instead of his expected rate of 30 per cent between 1900 and 1920, there was an increase of only about 17 per cent.

At any rate a large Negro group will be here for several centuries. Even an increase of one per cent every ten years would aggregate eleven and a quarter million Negroes by the end of the century. On the other hand, if it ever happens that deaths begin to exceed births to such an extent that the population decreases by two per cent every ten years, there will still remain, two hundred years hence, a colored population of about seven million; and if this decrease were maintained, a thousand years hence the race would still be more numerous than are the Indians to-day. In the meantime the persistent question of what to do to adjust the relationships of those who remain would continue to be vexing. That, rather than attempts to predict the future, is the pressing problem of to-day.

The birth rate among Negroes is evidently subject to fluctuations from a number of causes. This rate has undoubtedly decreased rapidly, and it is this decrease in birth rate rather than an increase in death rate which causes the slower increase of the Negro population. In fact, the following chapter shows that the death rate is declining.

One of the influential causes of the lower birth rate is the gradual rise in the standard of living. This postpones marriage until a later age than formerly and consequently reduces the number of children born. Nevertheless the marriage age is still very much lower among colored women than among white women, for the census indicates that 30 per cent of the white women over 15 are single as against only 24.1 per cent of the colored women over 15. In the city the birth rate is much lower than in the country, the rates per 1000 in 1920 being: urban 24.0, rural 28.9. The migration cityward, therefore, is another factor in the decreasing birth rate. The high incidence of venereal disease also serves as a check upon births, and it is also possible that conscious birth control has decreased the number of children to some extent. All these factors combine to reduce the number of Negro children born and to slacken the rate of the increase of the Negro population.

EFFECT OF NUMBERS

The present distribution of Negroes is one of the potent factors in determining race relations. In certain sections the sheer weight of numbers renders the task of racial adjustment far more difficult than in others. Mississippi and South Carolina, with over 50 per cent of their total population colored, present one set of situations, while the New England and Middle Western states, with less than 10 per cent, present a wholly different set. The situation in Georgia, Alabama, Louisiana, and eastern Arkansas is closely allied to that in Mississippi and South Carolina. North Carolina, Virginia, Florida, Tennessee, Kentucky, and Texas, where the proportion of Negroes ranges from a fifth to a third of the total population, present fewer difficulties.

The South has been looked on as "solid" in its views on the color question, but these variations of state situations are further complicated by a great variety of county situations. The "Black Belt" area, where Negroes are in the majority, extends from the tidewater of Virginia, down the coast of North Carolina, and spreads to include nearly all but the mountain counties of South Carolina. It then arches to the westward through Central Georgia, Alabama, and Mississippi, where it again expands north and south to include all the Delta counties along both sides of the Mississippi River in Mississippi, Arkansas, and Louisiana. A few detached "black" counties are to be found in Florida, Tennessee, and eastern Texas. In some of the Black Belt counties there are as many as ten Negroes to one white man. In such a county the attitude toward law and order, government, schools, health, and all phases of life is tinged by the color question to a far greater extent than in some of the counties of the same states where the ratio is reversed.

It therefore behooves the man who would deal intelligently with a local situation to know first the population conditions, the rate of increase, and the proportion of the two races. These are powerful influences upon the everyday dealings between the two races.

MULATTOES

The presence of a considerable number of people of mixed white and colored blood presents one of the genuine problems remaining in race relations. There is every evidence, however, that direct infusion of white blood through inter-marriage or illegitimate relationships is decidedly on the decrease. This evidence comes not only from competent observers of social conditions but also from census figures. Observers of social conditions are unanimous in the statement that miscegenation is by no means as common at present as before the Civil War, because the two races are not in such intimate contact and because public opinion in both races is decidedly more opposed to interracial immorality.

The census figures dividing blacks and mulattoes are not accurate, but such as they are, they show the following slight increases in the proportion of mulattoes in the Negro population, up to 1910. But from 1910 to 1920 both the actual number and the percentage of mulattoes decreased.

	1860	1890	1910	1920
Percentage of mulattoes in Negro population	13.2	15.2	20.9	15.9
Total numbers mulattoes	588,363	1,132,060	2,151,686	1,660,554

A slight percentage increase would be expected even if there were no direct infusion of white blood, since a mulatto child may be born to two mulatto parents or to one mulatto and one black parent, while a black child is born only to two black parents. On the face of the figures it is probable not only that the direct infusion of white blood has practically ceased, but also that the mulatto families are not as prolific as pure black families. Whether this is due to hereditary tendencies or different conditions of social environment has not been determined. Since the slight increase in the mulatto population is due to unions of black with mulatto and of mulatto with mulatto, it is probable that the proportion of mulattoes with more than half white blood is rapidly diminishing, while the proportion with less than half white blood is increasing.

MIGRATION

The curtailment of European immigration has left the Negro on the Southern farm as the largest available group of unskilled laborers in the United States, and this supply is slipping through the fingers of the Southern farmer because the latter is unable to compete with the manufacturer, either in wages paid or living conditions furnished. Each year after the crops are gathered and before the landlord has struck a new bargain with wage hands and tenants, many leave the farm and move cityward, putting behind them all that they have known to seek the Eldorado of industry.

When the pioneers arrive in the city they write back glowing accounts of the higher wages and more attractive life, thus drawing their friends after them. The movement then becomes an epidemic, a fad, and assumes large proportions. A story goes the rounds of one Southern town that an old Negro drove up to the station in an ox cart, with $37 in cash, saying that he was going to Philadelphia where colored people were as good as white folks and that he had brought his wagon along so he could ride when he got there. Many of the migrants do not have a much clearer idea of where they are going or why.

The Georgia State College of Agriculture estimates that about 100,000 people left Georgia farms from January 1 to May 1, 1923. Eighty thousand of these were Negroes. At times the "Jim Crow" cars of northbound trains are

packed to suffocation and the railway stations at Atlanta,
Memphis, Chattanooga, Cincinnati, Cleveland, Philadel-
phia, and other distributing centers present strange sights
of swarms of black immigrants, many of them clothed
almost as they left the cotton field, with all their earthly
possessions in one bundle.

There is a pathetic tinge to this picture of simple wan-
derers, many of whom really loved their homes with a kind
of "with all their faults I love them still" affection. Yet
they have been forced away by the combined action of a
faulty economic system and the social ills that attend it.
These have ground them as relentlessly as the upper and
the nether millstones.

It is well to bear in mind that this movement is no new
thing but has been in process ever since the slaves were
emancipated. Immediately after the Civil War it took the
form of a shift westward. This was so marked that a government investigation was instituted. A slow movement
northward has also been in progress for several decades.
It is only since 1910, however, that the movement has
become spectacular. The boll weevil's inroads on cotton
and the war conditions in industry have intensified it
greatly.

The striking increase in Northern cities since 1910 has
led many to look on the migration largely as a movement
from South to North. This is only a part of it. Fundamen-
tally it is a movement from the farms of the cotton belt to
the cities, and the rapidly growing Southern cities receive
as many migrants as Northern cities.

A picture of the plantation system will help in understanding the inability of Southern farmers to compete with

industries for labor. The one-crop system has always required a surplus of labor. From twenty-five to thirty acres in cotton and corn are usually cultivated by one man or family, but when a large proportion of this is in cotton, a surplus of labor is necessary to "chop" or thin the crop in the spring and to pick it in the fall. Thus the average number of days worked by the rural laborer in the cotton belt has been low. This is a wasteful procedure and has kept the level of wages low. The result has been that for the past fifty years there has been a gradual movement toward the higher wages of the city even in normal times.

But the years just before, during, and just after the European war were anything but normal in Southern agriculture. After a brief period of prodigal prosperity and equally as prodigal spending, the post-war depression, coupled with the ravages of the boll weevil, made matters decidedly worse. In many sections the farmers' cash and credit were exhausted and their morale was so low that the mere mention of financial outlay for improvements almost brought on apoplexy.

Large-scale production of cotton is carried on almost exclusively with hired labor or with share tenants, who are little more than laborers. These men are low in the industrial scale and poorly paid. Many are improvident and constantly in debt. They are, therefore, dissatisfied with their method of livelihood.

Their institutions are poor and rendered poorer because of their shifting constituency. The church, the school, and the lodge are the only plantation institutions. These fluctuate rapidly in attendance and support. There is little opportunity for developing any intelligent local leadership. One needs only to drive through such a section to note its drawbacks. For miles and miles the road stretches through plantations without a church or school. Then at some cross-road point, a miniature steeple upon a building little larger than a cabin proclaims it a church. Sometimes a small school and lodge hall stand near by. As often as not, church, school, and lodge use the same building. It serves for education during week days, for recreation a few nights in the month, and for worship at irregular intervals when the itinerant preacher gets around.

With unsettled population conditions, plantation houses are not homes; they are little more than temporary shelters where the laborer remains until the crop is made and then moves on. The traveler in the Black Belt is depressed with the desolateness of these isolated one- and two-room cabins, which stand in the cotton fields without attempt at decoration, with no garden, and even without any of the simple comforts of primitive country homes. They are often occupied by families of eight or ten people and four or five hounds.

To make matters worse, some planters persistently exploit their labor. Under the share-cropping system the temptation to do this is especially strong. The share tenant comes to the landlord with nothing but the clothes on his back and a few pieces of household furniture. For a period of eight or nine months, until the crop is made, he must be fed, clothed, housed, furnished with fertilizer, seeds, animals, implements, and stock feed. At the end of the year the crop is divided half and half after the tenant's expenses have been deducted.

Among the Negroes there are persistent complaints of unfairness in settlement at the end of the year. Some of these complaints are justified and some arise from the fact that the tenants are illiterate and keep no accurate accounts, and hence are uninformed as to their true financial status at the end of the crop year.

Much of the movement arises from this dissatisfaction with crop settlements. On the other hand, where a tenant or laborer moves in the middle of a crop year, he imposes a great hardship on the landlord, because he has been fed and financed by the landlord's advances made upon the sole security of a growing crop, which is dead loss if the tenant moves off in the middle of the season. Many landlords have been almost ruined in this way.

It is this situation which has given rise, in some states, to repressive laws aimed at the discouragement of migration. Among these are statutes making it a crime to quit a contract while in debt. Out of such laws peonage complaints arise. Another almost universal statute in the South is that aimed at labor agents, requiring the payment of a license fee of $500 to $1000 in each county in which labor is recruited and making it a crime to recruit labor without the payment of this fee.

As against these efforts to hold Negro laborers, there have been efforts to drive them out. These do not come from the landlord class, but from irresponsible members of the white tenant and small farmer group who are more or less in competition with Negro tenants. In several Southern counties Negroes have gone to worship on Sunday to find every church door placarded with the warning to all of them to be out of the county by a certain date. Such warnings have often been the work of practical jokers, but they have caused an abiding fear in the Negro who lives in isolated rural sections, especially when signed with the cabalistic initials K.K.K. In other cases law-abiding Negro citizens were whipped or otherwise terrorized by night riders and driven from home. Such cases have not been common, but have been widely discussed among the Negroes and have been a big factor in their unrest.

The result of all this economic depression, exploitation, and violence has been a great acceleration of the natural cityward movement. The 1920 census showed 3,559,000 Negro city dwellers, 1,550,000 of whom were in the North and West. There are now probably more than 4,000,000 in cities, over a third of the Negro population. It is estimated that over eleven thousand farms, aggregating 250,000 acres, were deserted in Georgia between January and May, 1923, and conditions are about the same in Mississippi, Louisiana, and Alabama. This means the loss of millions of dollars to Southern agriculture and a grave condition for the productivity of the country as a whole.

Despite their handicaps, however, Southern communities are making some progress in bettering conditions. They are taking steps which can be made more rapidly when prosperity returns to the farm. The most fundamental thing is that they are altering the farming system. The boll weevil and the labor shortage combine to make the planter discard the yoke of slavery to cotton and diversify his crops. By cutting down the cotton acreage and increasing the amount of winter grain, corn, velvet beans, peanuts, potatoes, cane, and peas, the planter can cultivate more land per laborer. Under this system more machinery is used also. On the whole, therefore, when the temporary ill effects of the suddenness of the movement have passed, the net result to Southern agriculture will probably be beneficial. The farmer will learn to be more economical with his land and labor, and will improve living conditions in rural districts.

Persistent effort is also being made to improve school conditions for Negroes. This is one of the big items in the mind of Negro leaders. From their observation of the benefits of the white man's learning, and as a reaction from the sting of former assertions that a Negro is incapable of learning, even the rank and file of the colored people have acquired a veritable passion for schooling. Recognizing this, numbers of Southern communities are building schools as fast as their means will allow. The Julius Rosenwald Fund for aiding Negro rural school building reports that within the past few years 2565 rural schools have been built at a total cost of $10,400,000, of which $5,680,000 was supplied from public taxes. In addition, many schools have been built without the aid of this fund.

As the realization grows that violence, and especially lynching, causes great unrest among the colored people, there is a marked increase in the determination of the thinking members of the community to bring to justice the perpetrators of violence and cure them of their practice. As far as the South is concerned, therefore, the movement of Negroes is virtually a strike against conditions, economic and social, which arise in Southern agriculture. The strike serves to focus the public mind on these conditions and efforts are made to improve them. Thus the movement of Negroes tends in the long run to improve both the economic and the social conditions in the South. As the Negro moves, his grievances are brought to light and an effort made to eliminate them.

The effects of this movement on industry are more or less obvious. On the eve of a wave of prosperity, when labor is needed for expansion, a source of cheap labor is opened up. Much of this labor comes right to the doors of the factory without recruiting. There can be no doubt that, compared with the non-English-speaking foreigners of former days, the Negro is a good industrial laborer. Until recently there was a rather persistent fiction in the South that the Negro was incapable of working with machinery. This has been disproved by the extent to which Negroes have been accepted and retained in the semi-skilled operations of the steel and automobile companies. In steel plants they rise as high as molders and occasionally as high as ruffers and rollers. The whole heat-finishing department of a large automobile plant is solidly Negro, and employers are constantly finding new uses in the skilled and semi-skilled operations to which this labor is adapted.

Another feature which appeals to many employers is that, as a rule, the Negro has been a non-union laborer. This is not his fault, since he usually joins the union when he can. Union labor, however, naturally looks askance on this influx of cheap, unorganized black men, and in many instances excludes them from their organizations. The American Federation of Labor announces a policy of non-discrimination, but the admission of members is entirely within the jurisdiction of each local union; and in many instances these unions exclude Negroes.

Upon the Negro himself the effects of this competition for his services are diverse. By moving North he obtains better wages, but these are almost balanced by immensely increased living costs. Probably his greatest advantage is in the superior living conditions of the city — better schools, churches, and recreation facilities, superior housing conditions and police protection.

If one considers the effects on the race as a whole, rather than only on individuals, the picture is more confused. The individual migrant looks to his immediate advantage, but when the long-time effects on family and group life are considered, immediate advantage is often outweighed by ultimate drawbacks. Among these long-range considerations may be mentioned the following:

From a home-loving, home-staying race the Negro has become the greatest wanderer among the restless groups of the United States. More than half the share tenants and laborers live on a place for one year only and then move. The 1920 census showed more than a fifth of the colored population living outside its state of birth. The enumeration showed 266,000 Virginia-born Negroes living in other states. Next in rank came Mississippi with 210,000, Georgia with 202,000, Alabama with 190,000, South Carolina with 169,000, North Carolina with 162,000, Tennessee with 147,000, and Louisiana with 115,000. Having lost their anchor the race is suffering many of the disadvantages of instability.

The crowding in cities has been one of the great causes of the decreasing Negro birth rate. Men and women are not equally attracted to any given community. Male agricultural laborers move to industrial cities. Women

are attracted to other cities by domestic service opportunities. In many of the Southern cities and in some of
those of the East the ratio of females to males is about 100
to 90, and in some cases as high as 100 to 80. In industrial
cities this is reversed. In Detroit the ratio is 137 men to
100 women, while in some small industrial towns it is almost
2 to 1. Thus by the arithmetic of population, hundreds
of colored men and women are destined to remain unmar-
ried. This is a fruitful source of immorality and crime, as
well as of reduction in the birth rate. Health conditions
in cities are also unfavorable to Negroes. Tuberculosis,
pneumonia, and infant diseases take a dreadful toll. In
fact, in some Northern cities the colored birth rate is less
than the death rate. In New York City between 1906
and 1916 the deaths amounted annually to about 400 more
than the births. In the absence of immigration these
places would show a shrinkage of Negro population.

Other adverse results of the cityward trend are seen in
the increased rates of crime, insanity, and dependency
among urban populations. Because the migrants plunge
from the simple, strictly-ordered life of the plantation
into the complex stresses and strains of the city, it is to be
expected that crime and insanity would increase. This has
been the case. When it is considered, however, that a
large proportion of the migrants are young and single, the
increase in crime and insanity rates has not been alarming.
A closer examination of colored crime records indicates
that many of the arrests are for minor infractions of city
ordinances.

As the migration settles down to a more normal and
steady stream, or as the industrial labor market becomes

saturated, these adverse effects of the stresses and strains of city life will doubtless be lessened. The ratio between the sexes will be balanced and the Negro will become more accustomed to city life.

The final test of the good or ill effect of migration on the Negro will be his ability to rise from the ranks of unskilled labor into the ranks of the semi-skilled and the skilled. If he is destined to remain a cheap, easily exploited labor group, then it would be far better for him to stay in his present recognized status in Southern agriculture and battle against its adversities for a more or less independent place as owner and renter of the soil. On the other hand, if there is room for a sufficient number to rise, then there will be an undoubted benefit to the race in the opening of this avenue.

While the influx of rural Negroes strains race relations in industrial centers, especially during seasons of unemployment, the dispersion of colored population is a blessing for the social situation in the Black Belt. In fact, the Black Belt proper—the area where Negroes are in the majority— is shrinking. Between 1910 and 1920 there was hardly a county in the South where the proportion of white people was not on the increase. In 1880 there were 300 counties with a Negro majority. In 1910 this 300 had shrunk to 264, and in 1920 only 220 of these remained. In 1910 there were 53 counties where the proportion of colored to white was more than three to one, but in 1920 only 32 showed such a high proportion. This scattering of Negroes from the predominantly colored neighborhoods lessens the demagogic talk of "Negro domination." At the same time it gives the Negroes more opportunity to learn from their white neighbors by observation than is possible when they live to themselves in masses.

In the long run, therefore, there is no cause for pessimism regarding the movement. The temporary ill effects on the Southern landlord and on the city-dwelling Negro show signs of adjustment, and as far as the Negro problems in general are concerned it is a great advantage that they should be spread and made nation-wide, rather than remaining intensified in the South.

BIBLIOGRAPHY

BOAS, FRANZ. The Mind of Primitive Man, pp. 274-278.

Census, United States. Negro Population in the United States, 1790-1915.

Also Census of 1920 Population.

EVANS, MAURICE A. Black and White in the Southern States, Chapter IX.

MECKLIN, J. M. Democracy and Race Friction, pp. 153-157.

MURPHY, E. G. The Present South, pp. 153-161.

PHILLIPS, U. B. American Negro Slavery, Chapters VIII, IX, and X.

REUTER, E. B. The Mulatto.

SCOTT, EMMETT. Negro Migration, Carnegie Foundation, Bulletin 16.

Special Bulletin of the United States Department of Labor, "Negro Migration in 1916-1917."

STONE, A. H. Studies in the American Race Problem, Chapter IX.

WILCOX, WALTER F. Probable Increase of Negroes in the United States. Published in Stone, A. H. Studies in the American Race Problem, pp. 496-530.

WOODSON, CARTER G. A Century of Negro Migration.

WOOFTER, T. J., Jr. Negro Migration, Introduction and Part II.

TOPICS FOR STUDY AND DISCUSSION

1. Make a study of the relative importance of birth rate, death rate, and immigration or emigration in determining Negro population increase in the United States and in some single state.

2. List the cities over 75,000 in 1890 and study their increase in Negro population. What effect has this had on the Negro race?

3. Study the census maps showing the percentage of Negroes by counties. Locate the "Black Belts." Locate the sections where there are comparatively few Negroes. What explanation can you give for this distribution?

4. To what extent is the Negro himself responsible for his presence in certain localities, and to what extent has his distribution been determined by the social and economic forces at work in the United States?

5. Outline the effects on a particular community of emigration or immigration of Negroes.

6. Discuss the causes of the declining Negro birth rate.

7. If the present rates of increase of the white and Negro populations continue, will their problems become more or less acute?

8. Discuss the steps taken in the South to retain colored labor.

CHAPTER IV

HEALTH

There is no other point of contact between the races where their mutual dependence is more real than in health matters. But in spite of the cardinal importance of health this phase of Negro life has not received as much attention as education, religion, and economic life. As long as both races use the same common carriers, streets, and public buildings, as long as one serves in the home, in the laundry, and in the stores of the other, disease in one race increases the chance of disease in the other. For, as Booker Washington expressed it : "A disease germ knows no color line."

If the white people but knew the surroundings in which their servants live and in which their clothes are laundered, the interest in public health work for colored people would be redoubled. Many who are careful of the surroundings of their individual servants have not realized the value of giving them protection by providing a healthy colored community in which they may live. It is not unusual to find cases of contagious diseases in the home of a domestic who spends her days in the kitchen of a white family.

There is a story of a white woman whose children had measles. When her laundress came she wished to be considerate and told her not to come any farther than the gate, explaining that if she came in she would carry the germs back and give them to her three children. The laundress exclaimed: "That's all right, my children have been having measles for a month." There was no need for either mother to have a further object lesson in the interdependence of their health conditions.

Increased attention to public health has lessened Negro sickness and death rates but they are still 50 per cent higher than white death rates. In the registration area in 1920 the colored rate was 18.4 per thousand and the white rate 12.8 per thousand. The Negro Year Book estimates that about 450,000 Negroes are sick all the time, that 225,000 Negroes die annually, and that 100,000 of these deaths and a large proportion of the cases of sickness are from preventable causes. The annual cost to the Negroes themselves for funeral expenses alone is $15,000,000, and the economic loss to employers is probably $300,000,000, of which $150,-000,000 is due to preventable causes. The Year Book therefore concludes that it would pay to spend $100,000,000 upon the improvement of Negro health. These figures measure the dollar loss alone and, of course, take no account of the useless suffering and anxiety which come from sickness and death.

CAUSES OF DEATH

When these causes of death are carefully considered it is evident that the Negro is dying principally of diseases which arise from filth, poor living conditions, and exposure. In other words, the Negro race is not greatly inferior to the white physically, but it lives under very inferior health conditions.

The principal causes of Negro death are as follows:

CAUSE OF DEATH	NUMBER OF DEATHS		RATE PER 100,000
	1920	*1921*	*1921*
1. Pneumonia and influenza . . .	23,396	11,183	107
2. Tuberculosis of the lungs . . .	18,029	16,467	157
3. Organic disease of the heart . . .	11,084	11,572	110
4. Acute nephritis and Bright's disease	8,660	8,682	83
5. Violent deaths (excluding suicide)	8,307	8,091	78
6. Congenital debility and malformations	6,166	7,364	70
7. Cerebral hemorrhage and softening	5,425	5,639	54
8. Diarrhea and enteritis	4,310	4,328	42
9. Cancer and malignant tumors . .	3,699	3,822	37
10. In childbirth	2,519	2,310	22

The table indicates that the colored people have their peculiar health problems which require especial emphasis in public health work. They suffer tremendously more from lung complaints than whites. The two leading causes given above, pneumonia and influenza, and tuberculosis, show a combined rate of 364 per 100,000. When it is also considered that whooping cough causes more infant deaths than measles, croup, and diphtheria combined, the prevalence of diseases of the respiratory system is further emphasized.

Several city health officers in Southern cities have maps with a black pin placed for each tubercular patient in the city. Often in some part of the colored section there is a cluster of these pins indicating as many tubercular cases in a small area as there are in all of the other sections of the city combined. This is usually in a lodging house section where the people are really below the poverty line and eke out their living by taking in one or two lodgers. Some of these houses have had cases of tuberculosis in them continuously for twenty years.

Excessive infant mortality in the colored population accounts for the death of between 10 and 15 per cent of the babies before they reach their first birthday. Valuable lives of young mothers are unduly sacrificed in childbirth. Here again are the results of ignorance and filth. The tenth cause in the table above is deaths in childbirth, showing a rate of 30 per hundred thousand in the total population. However, when it is considered that only women of child-bearing age are subjected to such deaths it is seen that the true significance of this rate is not apparent unless it is figured on the basis of women of child-bearing age, in which case it runs to about 100 per hundred thousand. The rôle of filth and ignorance is further emphasized by the fact that a third (877) of these deaths were from puerperal septicemia, or blood poisoning, which, in nearly every instance, is due to insanitary conditions in childbirth.

Here also the ignorance and superstition of the midwife, or, as she is often called, the "Granny," is evident. It has been estimated that in the rural South 60 per cent of the Negro women and about 12 per cent of the white women are attended in childbirth only by Negro midwives, without any advice from a physician. Until recently no systematic effort was made to instruct these women except in a few cities. Their craft was handed down to them by word of mouth from the previous generation. Their well-meaning but unskilled ministrations have many times resulted in needless death and deformity.

Although it shows in the causes of death only indirectly, the universal testimony of physicians is that venereal disease is also very prevalent among the colored people. The army figures also bear out the higher incidence of these diseases among the colored recruits. In the table above, this type of disease contributes to the high rate of death from organic heart troubles, nephritis, and Bright's disease and cerebral hemorrhage.

All of these principal scourges of the colored population yield readily to public health methods. It has been conclusively demonstrated that by the expenditure of time, effort, and money to segregate cases, disinfect houses, instruct the families of patients, secure proper ventilation, prophylaxis, and feeding, tuberculosis can be checked, infant deaths can be greatly decreased, the life of expectant mothers safeguarded, and the incidence of venereal disease greatly reduced. The answer to the Negro health problem is, therefore, education and more education, public health campaigns and more public health campaigns. The trouble in the past has been that too many communities have mapped out their campaigns of physical education and their public health programs without provision for the Negro.

RECENT IMPROVEMENT

But there is a brighter side to the picture. The health of colored people is improvable and is rapidly improving. Based on the experience and careful record of 1,500,000 policy holders of the Metropolitan Life Insurance Company, a recent very optimistic report by Dr. Dublin announces a striking improvement in Negro health during the past ten years. That this improvement is not an accidental thing and really reflects a thoroughgoing change in the mortality situation is indicated by the fact that the death rate has declined in every age period of life, and mortality from a diversity of conditions has been lessened. Among the very young children the death rate has dropped more than one half. Tuberculosis mortality has decreased from 418 per 100,000 to 244, or 42 per cent. Deaths from typhoid and malaria, which especially affect the rural districts, declined 75 per cent. In spite of the influenza epidemics, deaths from pneumonia have declined 26 per cent. Improvement along so many and diverse lines is most hopeful and indicates beyond a shadow of a doubt that the colored people have awakened to the importance of the health problem in their affairs. They have actually determined to profit by the opportunity to reduce the unnecessary loss of life from which they have suffered. If to this determination and increased activity on the part of colored people there can be added more organizations whose program wholeheartedly provides for public health work in the colored community much progress can be made in the next two or three decades.

But the difficulties may as well be faced first. These are two: First the ignorance of the mass of Negroes, especially those in rural districts. Second, the lack of organizations for spreading the health message. The traveler in the rural South is impressed with the poverty of the community life in many areas. Where the land is held in large plantations, tenant houses are scattered, villages are relatively few, and communication is poor. The only rural institutions are the church and the school, and these are widely separated, poorly equipped, and hampered by reason of their shifting constituency. Fifty per cent of the tenants live on the farm only a year and then move elsewhere. They are pilgrims, merely sojourning a while and lacking in interest in their community or its institutions and leaders.

CONSTRUCTIVE RURAL MOVEMENTS

As weak as the rural institutions are, however, they are the starting point of any program which would reach out and be effective in the country districts. By ignoring them too many county organizations have become units functioning only in the principal towns and lacking in constituency and influence in the villages and open country. The colored preacher and the colored teacher are the natural advisers and counselors of their people, even more so than white teachers and preachers are of white people, because their leadership is not divided with other classes as much as white leadership is.

Very little has been done so far to increase the interest of rural preachers in public health, but some distinct progress is being made with the teachers. The Anna T. Jeanes Foundation, in coöperation with the state and county school authorities, maintains supervising teachers in 250 Southern counties. These teachers travel throughout the county, aiding all rural teachers with their problems and bringing up the standard of the country school as much as possible. Within the past few years these teachers have been very useful in attacking the school health problems more systematically, and through the school they have affected the health problems of the community. This is a big field, however, and one in which much remains to be done. Entirely too many communities provide carefully for the medical inspection of white school children and ignore the black school children. Where epidemics are concerned, such a policy defeats itself, for an epidemic among the colored children will rapidly spread to the white schools and undo the public health work previously done in them. Any effort to reach the colored population with health programs must take into account these colored leaders, — the preachers, the teachers, and the farm and home demonstration agents.

Next in importance to the colored leader is the Southern employer. The living conditions on many tenant farms are such that hygiene and sanitation are strangers. It has been said of some of the houses that the school children can return home and study geology through the floor, botany through the sides, and astronomy through the roof. The landlords need to be impressed with the actual cash value of a healthy labor supply.

Much aid has been given to landlords by governmental agencies interested in better pigs, better mules, and better chickens, but, as yet, comparatively little has been done to help the farmer secure better labor. Within the past few years the farm and home demonstration agents have passed from a purely agricultural program to one which puts more stress upon farm health and sanitation. These are the strategic people for reaching the landlord. Comparatively few colored farm and home demonstration agents are now employed, but those who are on the job are demonstrating their worth in reaching their own people and influencing the sentiment of the employers.

These, then, are the elements in the community upon which to build: The present health organizations, the colored leaders, the farm and home demonstration agents, and the employers. The proper person effectively to focus all these efforts is the colored county nurse, whose duty will not be to do bedside nursing but to organize parents and teachers to follow up medical inspection of school children, to organize neighbors to do the home nursing work, to organize midwives into instruction groups and interest the doctors in clinics, especially venereal disease clinics, and secure the coöperation of the general health organizations of the county.

The voluntary health organizations which are represented by many local functioning branches in the South are the Red Cross and the National Tuberculosis Association. These have colored nurses in a number of cities but very few in rural districts. In many places a white nurse, employed by one or the other of these organizations, gives some time to work among the colored people.

Many counties are now ready for the services of such public health nurses if part of the funds could be supplied by a private source for beginning the experiment. For every one of the 250 supervising teachers now at work there should be a county nurse on the job. Here is a big field of public health work ripe for the harvest. There is great need for the interest and financial support of foundations for Negro health operating in the same way as the foundations now in the field of stimulating Negro education. These foundations supply aid to states in maintaining state supervisors of schools and they supply aid to counties in maintaining county supervisors and in developing strategic schools. There is nothing whatever to correspond to these agencies in the field of Negro public health, and in their absence it is difficult to persuade public authorities to appropriate public funds for colored nurses without a previous demonstration of their value.

Colored nurses, though working under established health agencies, will need aid in enlisting the interest and organizing the forces of the community. In order that this may be accomplished, an advisory body of white and colored citizens should be formed. The personnel of this body should represent the county and voluntary health organizations, the white employers, the educational boards, the farm demonstration forces, and the colored leaders. This board will provide the real team work which is so essential.

In many counties such advisory boards may be found already formed in the county interracial committees. Eight hundred of these county committees have been organized by the Commission on Interracial Coöperation. The primary object of these groups is to promote good will between the races, but they feel that good will is promoted best by working together for the good of the community. In a few places these committees are already backing health projects, and through their coöperation during the past three years National Negro Health Week has been more widely observed than ever before.

STATE DEPARTMENTS OF HEALTH

All of these community efforts for Negro health should be administered by efficient, sympathetic state, county, and city health departments. The beneficent influences of state campaigns against tuberculosis, venereal disease, maternal and infant diseases, and epidemics should be felt, as far as possible, by the colored people. Often they are the ones who need this work most. As the state departments of education employ specialists in Negro education, so the state departments of health should employ specialists in Negro health who can devote full time to organizing health projects among the colored people.

Other states would do well to emulate North Carolina, where a state colored tuberculosis nurse is employed, and Georgia and South Carolina, where colored nurses attached to the state departments aid the maternal and infant hygiene work among their people. These colored nurses are especially helpful in reaching midwives and organizing them for instruction.

The Georgia plan of carrying on the propaganda of the maternal and infant hygiene department is especially to be commended. This is done in a "Healthmobile," which carries clinical facilities into rural districts and divides its time between white and colored people. A colored nurse travels with the healthmobile and organizes her people for the examinations and lectures so that they may be most effective. Negroes are so set apart and different in their community life from white people that there is need for such special methods of reaching them with health messages.

A special function of state boards of health should be that of reducing the frightful mortality from tuberculosis. Educational campaigns should be planned to reach both colored and white people, and the clinical facilities should provide for both. Tuberculosis sanataria are important welfare institutions for the rehabilitation of these patients.

Only a few Southern states and counties make any provision for colored people in these sanataria, and the colored patients are, consequently, left in the community under the unskilled care of their families or neighbors.

HOSPITALS

The *Census of Benevolent Institutions* (1910) listed 325 general hospitals in the South, of which 195 admitted Negro patients. Many of these, however, have only a small Negro ward. There are 144 hospitals entirely for colored people listed in the Negro Year Book. These are, for the most part, small and poorly equipped. Many of them consist of only a few rooms fitted up by one or two colored physicians to accommodate their private patients. There are large areas in the South where Negroes are far removed from hospital facilities, and where it is often necessary for patients who are seriously ill to make long and painful journeys to reach a hospital.

There is much diversity of management and practice in these colored hospitals. Some are separate institutions, some are wards of city hospitals, some are operated by medical schools, and some are merely the adjuncts of private hospitals where one or two white surgeons can care for their colored patients. With the exception of the few separate hospitals, none of them provide facilities for young colored physicians to receive the practical hospital experience which is rapidly becoming a prerequisite for white doctors. In the colored wards of city hospitals and hospitals under white private management the internes and members of the visiting staff are in almost every instance white. Thus the patients receive the benefit of the superior skill of the white physicians, but in many instances the young white doctor is prejudiced and his lack of sympathetic interest in the patient offsets his skill. And besides, the Negroes are, to a large extent, shut off from the development of skill and experience which come from hospital training.

The development of hospitals in connection with the colored medical schools at Meharry and Howard has offered facilities for internes. In addition, there are a few other colored hospitals, such as those at Hampton Institute, Tuskegee Institute, and Talladega College. But the majority of Negroes in general practice are forced to open their own small hospitals or to turn their surgical patients over to white surgeons. The best interests of all concerned demand the extension of these facilities for training colored physicians as rapidly as possible, for the really well-trained physician is the logical person to attend his own people and to furnish the health leadership which is so greatly needed.

HOUSING

Something has been said already of the effect of rural housing on health, but the housing conditions in cities are even more menacing. For fifty years Southern cities have permitted the unregulated growth of Negro rental house sections which contain abominations to the eye and often to the nose. There is seldom any effort to enforce housing codes prescribing the size of dwelling, space between houses, and sanitary arrangements. A few houses are actually built without windows. The landlord's whim is the tenant's law and it is notorious that this type of rental property yields a higher per cent to the investor than any other real estate.

Adverse economic conditions segregate Negroes in the cheap, unhealthful, unsightly portions of cities. Their houses are in the alleys near the business section, in the hollows, the railway yards, and on the outskirts. Sanitary inspectors avoid these districts, and failure of the city to extend sewer lines into them often makes compliance with sanitary regulations an impossibility. It is not at all unusual to find areas covering many blocks where all the families pollute the soil by surface toilets, or where the canons of decency, as well as those of sanitation, are violated by fifteen or twenty families who use the same toilet. In the smaller towns this soil pollution is a serious menace, because the people depend upon wells for their drinking water.

The streets in these sections are usually unpaved and wholly lacking in garbage-removal facilities. These conditions are remediable and the money cost of the remedy is small in comparison to the saving in prevention of unnecessary sickness and death which would result. The fact that such conditions are permitted can, therefore, be attributed largely to gross ignorance and indifference on the part of the citizens of the community as a whole, and to gross inefficiency of the part of the city governments who permit a few penny-snatching landlords so to endanger the health of the whole town.

In the needed betterment of housing and living conditions the Negroes themselves have a large part to play. Their own standards of sanitary life need to be raised. This, of course, is increasingly accomplished through home ownership. The purchase of homes is one of the substantial signs of advancement of the race. In 1910 colored people owned 441,918 of their homes, and in 1920 this number had increased to 472,226, an increase of seven per cent in ten years. Many Negroes have a real ambition to own homes but are unable to finance the purchase.

A few Negro business men, from time to time, have met this need by building small homes and selling them on reasonable terms. All such ventures have been successful. There is no greater field for "five per cent philanthropy" than that open to the man who can finance the building of neat, comfortable small homes ranging from $2000 to $5000. These houses will sell on long terms and be disposed of rapidly, relieving congestion in crowded Negro districts and, at the same time, paying the builder a reasonable profit. The Service Realty Company did this on a large scale in Atlanta and Augusta.

The non-home owner also should be stimulated to develop a sense of responsibility for his sanitary surroundings and should be made to feel that he is a part of a community which will not tolerate insanitary spots. The increase of a general desire for better living conditions and a greater ability to maintain them among the masses will accelerate the efforts of municipalities to protect these living conditions by stricter housing codes, better streets, and more adequate removal of garbage and sewage.

RECREATION

The subject of health can hardly be dismissed without reference to the kindred subject, recreation. For proper relaxation is advocated as a preventive of many ills of both body and mind. Negroes are, however, woefully lacking in recreation facilities. Many of the school buildings have inadequate play space and practically none of those with space are equipped with play apparatus. Only one or two of the larger cities have parks or playgrounds for colored people. While they are a people naturally endowed with great sociability, the lack of means for getting together throws them back on commercial amusements, some of which are most vicious in character. Even though the commercial pool room and dance hall may be subject to grave abuses, there is little incentive to crusade against them when they are the only places to which the young people can repair for a few hours of amusement.

In their love for music the colored people have an urge to clean recreation which, with a little intelligent effort, could be utilized to great advantage. With only a little aid in providing meeting places, instruments, and directors, orchestras and choruses could be formed which would occupy much time pleasurably and profitably. It is customary in some towns for a colored chorus to give periodic entertainments in the open air at some central point where the whole community can enjoy the singing. Such a development of community music would not only enrich the musical life of the colored race but would enable the whole community to enjoy and appreciate their musical gift.

The only systematized efforts at wholesome recreation among the colored people are carried on by the Young Men's and Young Women's Christian Associations. The Negro Year Book lists 67 colored Y.M.C.A's of all types with paid workers. Many of these, however, are greatly hampered for lack of buildings or equipment. In 1910

Mr. Julius Rosenwald offered to pay $25,000 toward the cost of erecting any Y.M.C.A. building costing $100,000 or more and in 1920 he renewed this offer. Fifteen large city buildings were erected under the provisions of these offers. The International Committee of the Y.M.C.A. also carries on active student work in the colored colleges, and recently has begun to attack the high school problem. Sixty-four colored Young Women's Associations are listed, and this organization also carries on an active student work. In the case of both Young Men's and Young Women's Christian Associations, however, a disproportionate number of the organizations are in Northern states. The masses of Negroes in the rural sections and small towns are neglected in the matter of recreation.

Health, good housing, and recreation go hand in hand, and the general public has just begun to realize that to attend to public health work, better housing, and saner recreation for colored people is to lessen the load on the jails, the almshouses, and the hospitals, and to increase the happiness and efficiency of the laboring classes.

BIBLIOGRAPHY

DOWLING, OSCAR. The Negro and Public Health, Proceedings Southern Sociological Congress, 1912.

DUBLIN, LOUIS I. Reprint of address before National Urban League Conference.

HALL, GEORGE C. Negro Hospitals, Reprint from *Southern Workman* in 1910.

HOFFMAN, F. L. Race Traits and Tendencies of the American Negro.

The Negro in Chicago, Chapter V.

United States Census Vital Statistics and Reports State Departments of Health, Tuberculosis Associations, etc.

Young Men's Christian Association Year Book.

TOPICS FOR STUDY AND DISCUSSION

1. List the contagious diseases that are most likely to be transmitted from one race to another and look up the Negro death rate from each.

2. From the Negro Year Book describe the observance of National Negro Health Week, and discuss its possible benefits. Report on its observance in your community.

3. Study the housing conditions of a town or rural community, observing houses owned and rented, poorer houses, and better houses. To what extent are the Negroes themselves responsible for the conditions and to what extent are white landlords and sanitary officials responsible?

4. From the point of view of a local community, what is the effect of the following agencies on Negro health: State Department of Health, County or City Department of Health, Red Cross, Tuberculosis Association, National Social Hygiene Association, Hospitals? (If there is sufficient time, these associations should be written for reports bearing on Negro work.)

5. Report on the recreational facilities for Negroes in a community.

6. What benefits do the Negroes in your state derive from the Sheppard-Towner Fund (administered by the State Department of Health): (*a*) In maternal hygiene; (*b*) in infant hygiene; (*c*) in work among midwives?

7. To what conditions does Negro mortality seem to be due primarily?

8. What is the estimated economic loss from preventable disease among colored people?

CHAPTER V

PRODUCING ON FARMS

If agriculture in the South remains at the low ebb at which it has stood for several decades, its fate is sealed; and with it the fate of the United States as a self-sustaining, food-producing nation. Only for short periods of high prices has the Southern farm population been prosperous, and frequently in financial depressions and in long periods of low and medium prices, the farmer has barely made interest on his invested capital and has often suffered disaster. The condition of his tenants and laborers has been most unenviable.

The greatest asset of the South has been a world monopoly of cotton, without which the rehabilitation of the farms devastated by the Civil War would have been almost impossible. The necessity of profiting by this cotton monopoly has led to grave abuses in the agricultural system. Cotton was planted almost exclusively until the Southern farmer became dependent on others for his feed and foodstuffs. In a section whose rich soil and climate fitted it for growing a bewildering variety of crops, cotton usurped the field to a great extent. This process continued until the South became dependent upon the West for meats, upon the Middle West for mules and their feed, and upon the East for manufactured goods, fancy foodstuffs, grain and dairy products; and the Southern farmer paid a profit to the farmers of other sections and paid freight on long hauls, merely for the privilege of growing cotton. This progressed to such an extent that when the farmer attempted to diversify he found it difficult to market anything but cotton or secure credit on any other basis.

This dependence upon others for foodstuffs and the lack of adequate capital for financing farm operations have placed the Southern farmer in a poor bargaining position. To pay his debts he has been forced to sell his cotton in the fall, with the result that no monopoly price was exacted because he could not control the supply as monopolists do. The cotton profits have, for the most part, gone to the warehouseman, the speculator, and the manufacturer.

Southern Agriculture and Negro Labor

The predominance of Negro farm labor, — ignorant, improvident, and constantly shifting, — has had its part in fastening this system on the South; and the system, on the other hand, has had its grinding effect in keeping the masses of the colored farm population in sorely straitened circumstances. Any effort to improve these conditions of Southern agriculture must, therefore, take into account the improvement of the Negro; and likewise any effort to improve the Negro must take into consideration the improvement of the agricultural system of which he is a part.

From the beginning of colonial days the Negro showed adaptation to Southern agriculture to such an extent that the spread of colored population up to 1880 followed closely the cotton belt of the South. The physique of the race seemed more suited to the hot climate, and their ignorance and lack of skill bound the masses to farm labor. After three centuries of colored labor the mutual dependence of the Southern farmer and the Negro laborer has become traditional.

The importance of farm life in Negro affairs is indicated by the fact that 45.2 per cent are in agricultural pursuits. In spite of the twentieth-century shift to the cities, two thirds of the Negro population lives in rural districts, and many others in small towns are dependent for their prosperity upon the surrounding rural areas. The 218,000 Negro farm owners and the 193,000 renters represent the largest group of colored people who have attained economic independence.

On the other hand, the Negro is an important factor in the success of Southern agriculture. His bronze arms have, until recently, been almost wholly relied upon to till the fields of the Southern states, and the prosperity of the Southern farmer is built upon them. The tenant system, the credit system, the crop system have all taken their present form largely because of the predominance of the Negro in the field of agricultural labor. His presence discourages immigration and therefore has precluded the settlement of the South by groups of foreign-born farmers similar to those of the Middle West. Statistically this importance of the Negro to Southern agriculture is indicated by the fact that he cultivates 40,000,000 acres of land, an area twice as great as all the land in farms in the New England states, and he constitutes 40 per cent of all Southern agricultural workers.

Extent and Disadvantages of Tenancy

Since the Civil War many Negroes have become tenant farmers. At its close, 90 per cent of the Negroes were agricultural laborers. The census of 1920 showed over nine hundred thousand owners and tenants and a million and two hundred thousand laborers. In other words, there are almost as many tenants and owners as there are laborers. About half of these laborers are classified as working on the home farm. That is to say, they are the members of the families of farmers who are working at home, — serving an apprenticeship. Of the nine hundred thousand Negro farmers about two hundred thousand are owners and seven hundred thousand are tenants. This makes the total division of the Negro agricultural workers as follows: Laborers 57.5 (on home farm 25 per cent), tenants 32.4 per cent, owners 10.1 per cent. Coincident with the growth of the Negro tenant class has been the growth of a white tenant class, and the South has rapidly become a section of tenant farms. In 1920, 51 per cent of the farms were operated by tenants and only 49 per cent by owners.

The three principal types of farming are all to be found throughout the South. Some large tracts have been held intact by the owners and are cultivated entirely by hired labor. The decline of this type of farm is indicated by the fact that the average size of farm in the South has diminished from 153 acres in 1880 to 109 acres in 1920. At the other end of the scale is the small farmer, owning his own land and cultivating it with his family and some hired labor. Between the two is the tenant plantation, a large tract which the owner has divided among numbers of tenants either on a share or on a rental basis.

The tendency has been for the tenant areas to increase rather rapidly and the small farm areas rather slowly. This has occurred naturally in the breakdown of the antebellum plantations, which embraced a large part of the area

known to be fertile in 1870. While these plantations have
been breaking down into tenant farms, however, new lands
along the Coastal Plain have been cleared of timber, and
commercial fertilizer has rendered others cultivable so that
large new sections of labor and tenant plantations have been
opened up. The upper Piedmont counties of the Eastern
Seaboard states have always formed an area of small
farmers, and gradually, as the large plantations disintegrate,
small farmers have become interspersed throughout the
Black Belt.

It is to be devoutly hoped that this is only a temporary
condition arising out of the transition of the South from the
slave régime to that of freehold of the soil by the men who
cultivate it. Rarely in the world's history has tenancy
worked satisfactorily. The unrest of the manorial period
of England was an outgrowth of discontent of the tenants,
and its result was an intense land hunger which sent the
colonists to America in search of land which they could
own. Continental Europe, during the same period, seethed
with agrarian discontent; and much of the recent unrest
of agricultural sections of Europe has arisen from dissatisfaction with the division of the product between the landlord and the tiller of the soil. The present agricultural
troubles of the South are but signposts on the road to real
trouble in the future, if that future is to be one of tenant
farming on the present basis.

Tenancy is bad for the land because the tenant has no
real interest in permanent farming. He is there to make
money and to shift to other sections when his returns
diminish. As a result he mines the soil instead of farming it. John Stuart Mill quotes Arthur Young as saying:

"Give a man the secure possession of a bleak rock and he will turn it into a garden; give him a nine years' lease on a garden and he will convert it into a desert."

Share tenancy also reduces the product of the tenant, for, when he is fed and clothed on credit and receives only a half of the crop, he is not as ambitious or as energetic as he would be if he were working wholly for himself. It makes the scientific rotation of crops difficult because share tenant farming inevitably tends toward the production of crops which yield the highest money return. There is no encouragement to breed the farm animals which are so essential to the self-sustaining farm family. The tenant is not essentially interested in feed crops and the landlord is not interested in having his land used for production in which he does not share. The census of 1910 showed 396,000 colored farms with no cow and 308,800 with no hog. There are also hundreds of thousands of tenant farms without even a chicken. Many landlords do not properly encourage their tenants in the cultivation of a garden. Such neglect is short-sighted, because the cultivation of a garden and the breeding of domestic animals would furnish the tenant with food and reduce the amount which it is necessary for the landlord to advance to him to buy provisions.

In addition to these adverse economic effects, a flood of social ills follows the tenant system. The lower standard of living means a lower intellectual and moral standard, with corresponding indifference to religious and political development. Tenants move frequently and hence have no abiding interest in rural institutions, and in such a transient population rural leadership languishes.

For all these reasons a permanent tenant system is one to be avoided. When, however, the tenant is compared with the laborer, it is seen that his lot is the better. The laborer has less incentive to improve the land, less opportunity to cultivate a garden or raise domestic animals, less interest in, or attachment to, rural institutions, and receives a lesser portion of the harvest. The status of the share tenant and that of the laborer are, however, very similar. Whenever tenancy gains at the expense of ownership, therefore, it is a dangerous sign; when it gains at the expense of the number of farm laborers, however, it represents an advance. In other words, tenancy is a rung in the agricultural ladder whereby the landless, homeless man climbs into the ranks of the landowners. It will probably always remain to some extent as a transition stage between that of the young man on the home farm with no money and the independent landowning farmer.

RELATIONS OF LABORERS, TENANTS, AND OWNERS

As far as the Negro is concerned, the increase in tenancy represents a rise from the ranks of farm labor. This is evident because, at the close of the Civil War, all Negroes in agriculture were laborers. This increase has, therefore, not been at the expense of landownership. More white and colored landowners are reported at each successive census. The increase in colored tenants represents a transition of a number of colored farm laborers to the status of tenant. The progression from laborer to share tenant, to renter, to owner has not been steady with the masses. The average farm Negro is likely to go up and drop back, fluctuating as economic conditions change. Some get as high as renters, fail, and drop back to the status of laborers. A steady, industrious group has, however, climbed the tenant ladder into landownership. Whether the South remains predominantly a tenant section or not depends upon the ability of these tenants to take the second step and become landowners. Up to date this has been a slower process, but, in spite of the difficulties, 10 per cent of the Negroes engaged in agricultural pursuits have become owners of land.

Because the wages of farm labor are very low, fluctuating from $15 to $50 per month, the energetic man seeks to escape from the laboring class as soon as possible. When the colored farmer no longer desires to work as a laborer, he asks the landlord for a half-share contract. It is not necessary that he have money, because the landlord furnishes everything necessary for farming and even advances him money to pay for his food and clothing, and deducts these advances from the tenant's half at the end of the year. Under this arrangement the tenant gains or loses according to his success in raising the crop.

On the other hand, the landlord may make a high percentage on his investment in a share crop, for, if the tenant is successful, the landlord makes interest on his money, rent on his land, and a share of the profits in the enterprise. A study of farming in the Yazoo Mississippi Delta in 1913, made by the United States Bureau of Farm Management, revealed : That the income of the half-share tenant is lower but steadier and less subject to ruinous fluctuations than that of any of the other classes of farming population except that of laborers. In this respect they are much like laborers. The number of failures among share tenants is very low.

The average income is $333 (1913). Only 2.9 per cent earned less than $100 and only 5.1 per cent earned over $600. That the income of cash renters is still higher and still more subject to fluctuations. This class averaged $478 in income, but 9.8 per cent failed to make $100, while 28.2 per cent made more than $600. As the authors point out, "This difference is probably influenced but not entirely accounted for by the size of holdings."

From the point of view of the landlord the factor of income is reversed. His income from share-tenant farms yielded, on an average, 13.6 per cent on his investment. Where the share tenant's income is less than $100, however, the landlord's return is only about 3 per cent on his investment, but from share tenants with an income of over $1000, the landlord's yield is over 25 per cent. In the case of cash renters, the landlord's return was practically fixed at 6 or 7 per cent. The average is 6.6 per cent, the low range 5.7 per cent, and the upper range 8 per cent. Balanced against these differences in income is the fact that, in the case of third and fourth tenants and renters, the landlord not only furnishes less capital, but assumes a smaller risk than he does in dealing with share tenants.

It is comparatively easy to understand, from the financial point of view, why, in practically all cases where landlords can give personal supervision to their planting operations, they desire to continue the share-cropping system as long as possible. On the other hand, it is equally as easy to understand the natural desire of the ambitious tenants who have saved a little money, to "get up in the world" by chancing the greater gains of third and fourth cropping and renting even at the risk of a greater loss. Negroes with managerial ability who have accumulated a little money and who own their stock and implements, therefore prefer to operate as independent renters.

Growth of Negro Tenancy

In normal times this step from share tenancy to renting is very easily made. The Negro who has the reputation of being a good farmer can readily secure the credit for the necessary purchases, and, if he is thrifty and has good crops, he can pay off these loans in several years. In times of great farm prosperity, however, many landlords who rent out their lands during lean years, come back actively into farming and return to the share system. For this reason the 1920 census, taken at the peak of prosperity, showed a great increase in share tenants and decrease in renters. As a rule, however, with the exception of the period of 1910 to 1920, an increasing number of Negroes have been forging steadily up the agricultural ladder from laborer to share tenant, from share tenant to renter, and from renter to owner.

The following census figures show the extent to which this has been true:

TENURE OF FARMS OPERATED BY NEGRO FARMERS

	1920	1910	1900
Owners	218,612	218,972	187,797
Cash tenants	193,102	285,950	273,560
Share tenants	510,424	384,524	283,614
Managers	2,126	1,434	1,744
Total	925,708	893,370	746,715

In spite of the handicaps of the unprofitable agricultural system, the poverty of rural life, and the actual unfairness of some landlords, the Negro farmer has progressed to such an extent that Southern agriculture seems to offer the chief opportunity to work himself into a self-sustaining and respectable economic status.

THE DRIFT FROM THE FARM

Recent evidences, however, indicate that many rural Negroes have despaired of overcoming the handicaps and are deserting the farm. There were actually 700,000 fewer Negroes in agriculture in 1920 than in 1910. The slight decrease in Negro owners between 1910 and 1920 is truly alarming. It indicates that some owners actually sold out and joined the cityward exodus and that energetic men who otherwise would have become owners also deserted the farm. The decrease of 93,000 renters was due in part to the fact that the high prices of 1919 induced many landlords to refuse to rent their lands and to insist on the share-tenant arrangement. There were, however, many idle acres in the South to which these renters could have moved, but they either lapsed into share tenancy or moved into the city. This shrinkage in the number of Negro owners and renters indicates the startling probability that colored people are losing what has been their most hopeful opportunity, or rather trading a most hopeful agricultural opportunity for a rather problematical position in Northern industry.

Any one reasonably familiar with the situation in the South can but feel that if this drift from the farm to the city should continue until the Negro loses his hold on the soil it would be a great disaster to the race and a misfortune for the South. While some scattering of the Negro population is beneficial, the continued movement of the better class of Negroes would be a misfortune to the South because the self-sustaining Negroes on the farm make a real contribution to the South's economic strength and present fewer problems of health and morals than do the city dwellers. It would be a calamity to the race because so large a proportion have made a start toward success in agriculture and have thus earned for themselves a respectable standing in the community. Again there is less competition and consequently less racial friction in agriculture than in any other line of work.

The growing tendency to diversification of crops and improved agricultural methods is undoubtedly greatly improving the economic status of the Southern agricultural worker. The improved economic conditions will be attended by better roads, better churches, better schools, and, in short, a richer life for the rural people. The forces of Christianity and Democracy are also at work to improve race relations, to secure greater protection and juster treatment of colored people in rural districts. These tendencies indicate a bright outlook for the colored man in agriculture, especially if, through good management, he can rise through the tenant class into the ranks of the independent farmers and can make friends in his community. To such a class agriculture offers an opportunity of living and rearing a family comfortably in surroundings where morals and health are good and educational advantages constantly improving, in a land where generous nature has provided all that man requires for prosperity and happiness.

A British traveler in the South became most enthusiastic over the agricultural opportunity of the Negro as compared to that of the natives of British Colonies.

Judging by the standards of the producing British Colonies land is cheap; judged by its possibilities it is very cheap. This means that if he (the Negro) liked to take to agriculture he could at once purchase and stock a small improved farm or a larger unimproved one, and raise enough in a very few years to return the purchase price. Such a man need never be in debt. He could buy his requirements and sell his produce on the very best terms, as well as any white man, and yearly improve his holding and add to his possessions. — M. S. Evans, "Black and White in the Southern States," pp. 248–249.

The fact that larger numbers of Negro farmers have not taken advantage of these opportunities is due, in a great measure, to their lack of training in thrift and inability to overcome the difficulties which arise from the one-crop system. These difficulties which confront the Negro are real and need to be recognized.

Laxity in Tenant Agreement

The first difficulty arises from the laxity of the business methods employed in the share-cropping operations. The ignorant and thriftless share tenant comes to the landlord with nothing but the clothes on his back and has to be housed, fed, clothed, provided with stock, feed, seeds, and fertilizers until the harvest can be gathered. After the crop has been divided into shares, the loans to the tenant for his maintenance are deducted from his share before it is turned over to him. In nine cases out of ten there is no contract, — merely a verbal agreement. Often neither the landlord nor tenant keep strictly accurate accounts, both depending upon the preservation of receipts or store accounts to keep track of debits. This laxity leads to discontent with settlements. Some landlords willfully take advantage of their tenant's ignorance and helplessness and appropriate his share of the crop as well as their own. When the tenant has no contract and keeps no records he has very little chance of recourse to the courts. Such landlords who "farm their Negroes rather than their land" are by no means in the majority, but there are enough of them in many communities to keep alive a spirit of discontent and resentment among the colored farming population. Their presence in a community makes it harder for the honest, fair-dealing men to secure contented laborers and tenants. As often as not the tenant is discontented with his settlement even though he has been justly dealt with. When he keeps no records and is extravagant in his purchases of food and feed, and when his crops sell for less than he expected, he often feels that he should have more than his share actually amounts to. This dissatisfaction with crop settlements is a potent factor in the unrest of the Negro rural population and needs the constructive attention of those genuinely interested in the advancement of Southern agriculture.

As Dr. W. E. B. DuBois, a keenly observant Negro student, puts it:

A thrifty Negro in the hands of well-disposed landlords and honest merchants early became an independent landowner. A shiftless, ignorant Negro, in the hands of unscrupulous landlords or Shylocks, became something worse than a slave. The masses of Negroes between the two extremes fared as chance and the weather let them.

It is obvious that the Negro himself can do much to remove himself from the position in which he can be imposed upon. In the first place no one but the share tenant is in such a position, and the thrifty, hard-working farmer can rise from the share tenancy to renting or ownership. In the second place study and application on the part of the share tenant will enable him to keep his own accounts and safeguard himself from exploitation. Passage of laws to the effect that no tenant contract is enforceable unless it is written would also help this situation, and the custom of keeping a memorandum account book for each tenant would help clear up crop settlements.

Many economists feel that tenancy will always be more or less prevalent. They reason that the pressure of the population upon food supply tends to send the price of land up to the point which discourages ownership. At any rate tenancy will be a factor in the agricultural situation and in the task of racial adjustment for many generations.

Is it not, then, the wise thing to turn for guidance to countries, such as England, where legislation has mitigated the evils of tenancy both for the tenant and for the landlord? One most worth-while reform inaugurated in England is in the reimbursement of tenants for permanent improvements which they make on the land. It is to the advantage both of the tenant and the landlord that the tenant treat the land as if it were his own; that he build the necessary fences and terraces, improve the farm buildings, and drain the swampy places. Under the present system he has absolutely no incentive to make improvements. But if, when he moved, he could, by law, demand reimbursement for unexhausted improvements, then he

would be encouraged to make these improvements. Such
laws, coupled with a concerted effort to create among the
tenant classes a desire for more permanency and more
progressive farming, would greatly mitigate the evils of
tenancy.

RURAL CREDITS

The second great difficulty faced by the Negro is the
iniquitous credit system which has grown up with the
tenant system. The South is continually one year behind
with its finances and has been so for fifty years. When the
Civil War wiped out all capital except land, the Southern
farmer formed the habit of borrowing to finance his operations and giving as security a mortgage on his growing crop.
Many of them have never yet caught up, and each year,
when the crop is planted, they borrow at a high rate of
interest to pay for their feed, fertilizers, seeds, and implements. The fact that the one-crop system has made the
farmer buy so much foodstuff which he should produce at
home has made this credit burden all the heavier. The
shiftlessness and lack of thrift of the mass of Negro tenants
has cemented the burdensome system so that each year a
greatly disproportionate part of the money of the farmer
and the tenant goes to the banker and the supply merchant
as interest. This high rate is charged as a matter of protection. The risk involved in such loans is great, for a crop
failure often means the loss of the money. No one can
blame the banker and the merchant for protecting against
such loss, but the fact remains that the resulting high rate
is a great burden to the farmer. The employment of so
large a proportion of the South's mobile capital in these
loans and the necessity of bringing in capital from other

sections has fixed a high rate of interest. The rate in the South averages from two to three per cent higher than that in the East and Middle West. In this respect the lack of thrift of the farmer and the resulting rotten system of agricultural credit acts as a drawback to Southern industry, burdening it also with the high interest rate fixed by the crop-loan system.

It was not until recently that a farmer could conveniently secure long-time mortgages on his land and escape from the crop-lien system. Capital was too scarce and too well occupied in reaping high rates from crop liens and supply accounts to be employed in land mortgages. As Southern banking developed, many large city banks have opened farm-loan departments, but many of these make it a flat rule not to lend to Negroes. While there is some justification of this on the ground that fewer Negroes are thrifty farmers and these are subjected to greater difficulties than white farmers, still such an arbitrary policy seems short-sighted on the part of the banking interests, for there are numbers of Negro farmers who, with a small mortgage loan, could escape from the credit system and pay their debts in a few years. The refusal of the banks to develop this business will inevitably result in its development by Negro banks, just as the flat refusal of the majority of insurance companies to write Negro insurance has resulted in the development of large Negro insurance companies.

The Federal Farm Loans could be of much assistance in this connection if it were not for the fact that prejudice militates against the Negro here also. These loans are not individual loans but are made to groups of farmers who apply through a local agent. In many communities a

Negro finds it difficult if not impossible to gain entrance to one of these groups. There are, however, a few Negro associations.

PEONAGE

The third pitfall which besets the thriftless and disadvantaged Negro is that of peonage, — a condition in which some Negroes are held in semi-slavery to work out a debt which is seemingly never satisfied. Only the unsuccessful who contract a debt to a particularly unscrupulous landlord fall into this condition, and many Southern communities are entirely free from peonage cases. Still, there are a sufficient number of cases which go uncorrected by public sentiment in some communities to cause abiding discontent among the colored people.

One form of peonage arises naturally from a set of laws passed to protect the landlord's legitimate interests. For years after the Civil War the Negroes were unreliable and unstable. It was not an uncommon occurrence for a landlord to feed them halfway through the crop year only to have them move off and leave his crops to the mercy of the weeds. To protect against this, laws were passed making it a misdemeanor to quit a contract upon which advances had been made. Under the letter of this law the laborer or tenant quitting such a contract should be brought back and lodged in jail. Practically, what often happens is that he is brought back and put on probation to his landlord, or fined and compelled to work out his fine by the landlord, who pays the fine. Sometimes when the minor officers of the law connive with the landlord, tenants are brought back on warrants charging them with some trivial offense such as "stealing corn," "stealing one plow line," or "stealing a chicken." Occasionally these warrants are not even returned to the issuing officer and the tenant is merely put back to work under threat of jail. At other times he is fined and made to work out the fine. As has been said, this is not common. The majority of Southern landlords deal fairly and treat their tenants as well as the agricultural system will permit, but there are cases of flagrant peonage and there are communities which wink at the practice and whose society welcomes the possessors of fortunes made in this way.

Here again greater education and more thrift will lift the Negro above the plane where he can be imposed on in such a manner. But the pressure of public sentiment of white people should also be exerted against such disgraceful practices. Social boycott would be too mild a penalty for the man who indulges in such exploitation. Without this pressure of public sentiment on the part of decent people in the community it is difficult, even in the federal courts, to convict men of peonage. The federal government could, however, do much more than it is doing to destroy this practice if the Division of Investigation of the Department of Justice adopted the policy of assigning men the special responsibility of running these cases down instead of waiting until such cases are reported to them. The evidence in some cases is flagrant enough, and only a few convictions in each state would be necessary to bring about a marked crystallization of sentiment against the practice.

Farm Demonstration Agents

The greatest constructive force in the Southern rural districts is the farm and home demonstration service.

These county demonstration agents are in direct contact with the farmer, the farmer's wife, and the rural school children; and their messages of diversification, rotation of crops, and improved methods of cultivation are inspiration carried directly to the farm. Their corn clubs, pig clubs, poultry clubs, and canning clubs are the most concrete and stimulating projects of agricultural education which have ever been conducted.

This type of training is greatly needed to enable those Negroes who do remain in the South to make a decent living from the soil. Yet, comparatively few Negro agents are employed, and the white agents have their hands full to care for the white farmers in their counties. There are 220 counties in the South in which Negroes are in the majority, and more than 500 others where they form a considerable proportion. In each of these a colored agent would more than pay for himself. At present only about 250 of the 1700 demonstration agents are colored. There are fully 400 other counties which need such agents. South Carolina with 109,000 Negro farmers in 33 counties has only 7 agents. The largest number in any state is to be found in Alabama, where the 95,000 colored farmers are served by 37 agents. These men are financed partly by state and national appropriations and partly by the county. The difficulty arises in getting county officials to provide for colored agents. Funds are available from the state and federal appropriations whenever the county provides its share.

The provision of credit, improvement of rural institutions, and the education of the farmer through agricultural schools, and through the work of the demonstration agents are all tasks of vital importance to the South. For, it matters not how many Negroes may leave the farms, those who remain need aid in order that they may make a respectable living from the soil and build progressive rural communities.

BIBLIOGRAPHY

BAKER, R. S. Following the Color Line, Chapter IV.

BANKS, E. M. Economics of Land Tenure in Georgia.

BIZZELL, W. B. Farm Tenantry in the United States.

BROOKS, R. P. The Agrarian Revolution in Georgia.

Bulletins, States Relations Service, United States Department of Agriculture.

Census, United States. Negro Population, 1790–1915, Chapter XX. Census, United States. 1900, Bulletin, #8.

DuBois, W. E. B. *Bulletin of the United States Department of Labor*, "The Negro Landholder in Georgia."

EVANS, MAURICE S. White and Black in the Southern States, Chapter XXVII.

JONES, T. J. The Negro and the Census of 1910. Reprint from *Southern Workman*.

PHILLIPS, U. B. American Negro Slavery, Chapters XII and XIII.

STONE, A. H. Studies in the American Race Problem, pp. 81–125.

TAYLOR, H. C. Decline of the Landowning Farmer in England.

United States Bureau of Education, 1916. Negro Education in the United States, Vol. I., Chapter VII.

WASHINGTON, B. T. Story of the Negro, Chapter II.

WOOFTER, T. J., JR., and FISHER, ISAAC. Coöperation in Southern Communities, Chapter III.

WOOFTER, T. J., JR. Negro Migration, Part I, Chapters I, III, and IV.

TOPICS FOR STUDY AND DISCUSSION

1. What is the relation of farm tenancy in the South and in other sections? (See Bizzell, "Farm Tenancy in the United States," pp. 117–127, and United States Census of Agriculture.)

2. What changes in relation to white neighbors have been caused by the growth of tenancy and ownership among Negroes?

3. Discuss the relation of the Negro farm owner to the community. Is his status desirable?

4. Review the discussion of migration in Chapter III and discuss the relation of farm tenancy to migration.

5. What can the Negroes themselves do to better their agricultural status and what aid can be extended to them?

6. Enumerate the factors in which the interests of the tenant and landlord are in harmony.

7. If you are familiar with a town where Negro farmers trade, report on the following conditions: Is there a difference in cash and credit prices charged by merchants? What interest is charged on open accounts? What interest on mortgage loans? If you are in a city, secure opinions on these points from bankers.

8. Study a county to determine the extent to which Negroes enter into coöperative movements; (*a*) to control farm pests; (*b*) to promote coöperative buying; (*c*) to promote coöperative marketing.

CHAPTER VI

PRODUCING IN CITIES

Though agriculture has long been of dominant importance in the economic life of the Negroes, there have always been a few in the skilled trades. All the stately ante-bellum mansions of the South stand as monuments to the skill of Negro carpenters and masons. Many slaves purchased their freedom by the practice of a craft. Soon after emancipation a few began to drift cityward, and when the great European war opened the door of opportunity to all who could work, many more Negroes moved to town. The 1920 census showed 3,000,000 of these city-dwelling colored people. These men traverse the whole scale of American life. Common laborers and domestics form the largest proportion, but there are a number in the skilled trades and quite a few in the professions and in business. In short, colored leadership in professional and financial lines, like the leadership of the white population, is centering in cities.

The manner in which these city dwellers earn their living tells two things. It indicates the extent to which they influence the productivity of the cities, especially Southern cities, and it shows the rate at which Negroes have been able to rise in the economic scale and demonstrate an ability to produce goods and services which they can exchange for a respected position in the community. In other words, the occupations of Negroes are an index of their value to the city and of their ability to do things for themselves.

Comparison of the census of occupations of 1920 with the census of 1910 shows significant changes in colored occupations in the past ten years.

NUMBER OF NEGROES TEN YEARS OF AGE AND OVER
GAINFULLY EMPLOYED

OCCUPATION	1920		1910
	Number	Per Cent	
Agriculture	2,178,888	45.2	2,893,375
Mines, quarries, manufacturing, and mechanical	960,039	20.0	692,506
Domestic and personal service . .	1,064,590	22.0	1,122,231
Transportation	312,421	6.5	255,969
Trade	140,467	2.8	119,491
Public service	50,552	1.0	22,382
Professional	80,183	1.7	67,245
Clerical	37,011	.8	19,336

Thus the amazing shift from agriculture commented upon in the previous chapter stands out. It is to be remembered that in 1865 Negroes were nearly all employed in agriculture. In 1920, for the first time less than half the Negroes were employed on the farm. Domestic service shows another slight decrease but still occupies almost a fourth of the colored people. Another fourth is engaged in mining, quarrying, manufacturing, mechanical, and transportation pursuits, while a bare twentieth are scattered in the other occupations.

DOMESTIC SERVICE

In point of numbers domestic service occupies more than any city occupation and includes nearly a fourth of all colored people. Here the contacts between the races are most numerous, and these contacts are so intimate that they have great weight in determining race relations. The Black Mammy affection of the past generation arose from these contacts, and much of the friction and impatience of the present day arises from inefficiency in the kitchen, in the laundry, or in nursing duties.

These domestic service relations have changed greatly since the Civil War. In slavery the highest types were hand-picked for domestic service, and, as "dwellers in the big house," they were the aristocrats of the slave plantation. When freed, however, it was natural that these more able and more advantaged Negroes should become the leaders of their people. The women married and remained at home and the men became the preachers, teachers, and business men. An intermediate class became the skilled and semi-skilled workers and a low class was left in domestic service. The wages paid these servants are considerably below the scale paid servants in other parts of the country, which is an additional reason why only the untrained are attracted to service.

Many good housewives receive all their impressions of the Negro race through contacts with their own house servants. Much misinformation about the race is gathered from this low-class element. A rise in the standards of the colored servant class would go far toward restoring some of the strong affection which existed between the races at the

South in ante-bellum days, and which has been immortalized in the literature of the period.

The present output of schools giving specialized domestic science courses is, however, hardly adequate to supply the demand for teachers of this subject in the public schools. The actual effect of these courses upon work in the kitchen has, therefore, been indirect. It has come through the public school pupils who have received a smattering course. Some successful efforts have been made to train cooks on the job in night and afternoon classes. This activity is one which should appeal strongly to public school authorities. As yet, however, only a few of the colored schools are supplied either with teachers or equipment to handle such classes successfully. In the few cases where these extension courses have been offered to cooks, both the servants and the housewives have been well pleased with the results.

Because character is so strong a factor in training for domestic service, there can be no hope for a rapid improvement in the average domestic until the general level of the family life of the masses is raised. For this reason housewives should be far more solicitous as to the home and neighborhood conditions in which their servants live. The effect of domestic service contact on race relations is so direct that the improvement of the character of domestic service is also worthy of the careful attention of Negro leaders.

One of the distressing features of domestic service is that young women are sometimes lacking in adequate moral protection. Their hours are long and they are away from their homes a great part of the day, often returning late at night. Married women with families also hesitate to enter domestic service because the duties keep them away from home all day. It is not at all uncommon to see little tots on the street locked out of the house for the day while the mother is away at work. Often a mere baby of a few months is left in the charge of a child only a few years old. Sometimes they are locked out and exposed to all the dangers of the street and sometimes they are locked in and exposed to the dangers of a sudden fire. In either event their chances for health and morality are greatly impaired and under this haphazard relationship they grow up hardly knowing the meaning of the word mother.

This situation could be mitigated by the erection of day nurseries and kindergartens. Very few Southern public school systems have colored kindergartens, and the development of day nurseries has not received the aid which it deserves from Southern housewives. A notable example is furnished by the Gate City Free Kindergarten Association of Atlanta. For a number of years a group of progressive and unselfish colored women who felt this need have supported three free kindergartens in neglected settlements. Two rooms, a worker, and some play apparatus constitute the necessary equipment. As the public schools assume the kindergarten activities, the institutions are converted into day nurseries for the younger children. It is only very recently that this band of colored women have received from white people any material aid in this project which is of distinct benefit to the whole community.

The great need is that domestic service be made more of a vocation and regarded as such by the housewife. The women's section of the Commission on Interracial Coöperation recommended that "all necessary steps be taken to insure the health and cleanliness of those who engage therein and to provide adequate safeguards for the moral protection of the girls and women who make their homes on the premises of their employers." This care on the part of employers, together with greater emphasis from Negro leaders on the value of character in domestic service, more effort to develop training courses in domestic science, and to develop kindergartens, day nurseries, and playgrounds will all reflect in improvement of the colored domestic.

WOMEN IN INDUSTRY

Between 1910 and 1920 there was a shrinkage of 440,000 in the number of women engaged in agriculture and a small decrease in the number engaged in domestic service. The great majority of this half million women have married and found homes in which they can remain and devote their attention to rearing families. Some of this loss in agriculture and domestic service, however, is offset by the entrance of colored women into industrial pursuits.

The European war and the post-war expansion in industry opened lines of industrial opportunity to colored girls as it did to white girls. Up to 1910 only 10,467 colored women were listed in trade and transportation and 81,258 in manufacturing and mechanical pursuits. By 1920 a remarkable increase was shown. The number in each group had doubled.

An investigation made by the United States Department of Labor in 1919 showed that these women were working at many different processes and under very different working conditions. The Report of the Chicago Commission on Race Relations, made at the peak of the labor demand in

1920, showed many more women at work in industry than in 1910. The principal increases had been in sewers and sewing-machine operators, slaughtering- and packing-house operatives, box making, tanneries, clerical occupations, and laundries. A few months later, however, in a period of industrial depression, many of these women were not retained. The commission reports :

Women's work presents a very discouraging outlook. Hundreds of needle workers are out of employment by the closing of many of the smaller shops which employed colored girls. Immigrant white girls are said to be consuming much of the work offered to domestics. Colored women seem, in most cases, as reluctant as ever to accept domestic employment.

In summarizing its report the Department of Labor Bulletin stated :

So far as the situation may be regarded as peculiar to the Negro woman, it may be said that she has been accepted, in the main, as an experiment. Her admittance to a given occupation or plant has been conditioned upon no other workers being available, and her continuance frequently hinged upon the same. She was usually given the less desirable jobs. The Negro woman worker, being new to industry, has to learn the lessons of routine and regularity. The attitude both of the employer and of the other workers toward women workers was one of uncertainty.

At best therefore, the position of Negro women in industry is precarious in the North. In the South they are rarely employed in industries managed by white people except in laundries, tobacco factories, and peanut-product factories. There is one overall factory in Atlanta which has, for some time, operated entirely with colored women workers. The management is pleased with the results. The increasing number of Negro businesses offer a field for ambitious young colored women as well as young men. Banks, toilet-goods companies, and insurance companies have a growing army of employees.

Up to the present time the problems of shop management seem to have constituted the chief bars to the progress of the colored woman in industry. Difficulty in mixing colored and white women employees, difficulty in securing able and sympathetic supervision, and difficulty in arranging suitable working conditions, such as dressing rooms, toilets, housing, and recreation, make the task of utilizing colored girls complicated. When these difficulties are obviated, the experience of employers on the whole appears to be that the services of colored women are satisfactory.

For a well-educated or skillful girl to be forced to work as a domestic or remain idle no doubt involves a great economic waste which could be conserved by judiciously developing opportunities for the employment of colored women in industry. The entrance of numbers of older women into industry is, on the other hand, a tendency to be discouraged because the colored people, even more than the white people, need home-makers, women who can remain away from the factory and devote their attention to rearing moral, intelligent, and thrifty families.

Unskilled Labor

The Negro unskilled laborer is constantly in demand in both Northern and Southern cities. Of the million three hundred thousand in mining, manufacturing and mechanical pursuits, transportation, and public service, over a million are unskilled. Here one finds the chronically "worthless" city Negro and here also is the ambitious man who moves in from the country without a trade and subsists on so-called "common labor."

These two types are widely divergent and deserve separate treatment. Too often the whole Negro race is indicted for the shortcomings of the worst type of shiftless day laborer. This class makes up a small proportion of the whole, but weighs heavily on the feelings of the employer, to whom it is a constant source of irritation. This worthless class works when hungry and when filled cannot be made to work either by offer of reward or threat of arrest for vagrancy. They may be seen for several days digging in the streets; after spending their earnings, they turn up in a railroad gang; next they may try some of the heavy construction work. They are contented with little and have little. They are floaters, and their class furnishes the labor turnover which is the bane of the boss's life. Some manage to live partly off the wages of hard working women and thereby shun the indignities of labor for many weeks at a time.

That this class forms a small proportion is indicated by the fact that the Negro has proved so satisfactory in Northern industry and in certain fields of Southern industry. The 1919 study of the Department of Labor showed that, in unskilled units, the Negroes worked more hours per week than white workers in nearly one half the units, the same in about one fourth, and less in about a fourth. In answer to the question as to whether or not Negroes were ambitious and desired advancement, sixteen employers said "yes," five said "not in all cases," five said "a few," and eight said "not as a rule." The exhaustive report of the Chicago Commission on Race Relations concludes that "Though ill-fitted for the keen competition, business-like precision, and six-day-week routine of Northern industry, the Southern Negro, in spite of these handicaps, has succeeded in Chicago." On the question of efficiency seventy-one employers reported their Negro workers equally as efficient as the white, and twenty-two considered them less efficient. As to absenteeism, fifty-seven expressed an opinion that absenteeism was no greater among Negroes than among whites and thirty-six reported that it was greater. Twenty-four felt that the labor turnover was the same among the Negroes as among the white employees and twenty-eight reported a greater turnover among Negroes.

In short, all the investigations that have been made seem to indicate that the attitude of the foreman goes a long way toward determining the efficiency, regularity, and steadiness of Negro labor. A sympathetic foreman who knows how to get along gets steady and efficient service, while in the case of a prejudiced foreman the colored worker responds with grudging and irregular service.

Although the years of the World War, and the years immediately following, were periods when the pressures and rewards for labor were very high, still the measurable success of the Negro worker shows that the loafers were in the small minority in the industrial centers. There are probably a larger number in the small towns of the South where the population is recruited fresh from the surrounding country, where labor is still casual, and where the requirements for subsistence are less stringent.

Quite aside from any temporary effects of high wages or high prices, there are two sets of forces which conspire against the "professional loafer," and which have tended greatly to increase the proportion of steady, conscientious colored workmen. The most important comes from the steadier groups of the Negro population. Increasing morality makes it more difficult for the loafer to receive financial aid from women through sentiment. More education and the resulting rise in the standard of living make it harder for him to keep up appearances without labor; and a change in the attitude of Negro leaders, a growing insistence upon sobriety and industry as the hallmarks of respectability, puts upon the idler an increasing social pressure.

Booker Washington's insistence upon the dignity of labor has had much to do with this change. At the time when he staked his chances for the leadership of his people upon this philosophy it was a courageous thing to do because the masses of Negroes had learned to associate labor with slavery and believed that, by some mysterious process, emancipation had freed them from an ignominious necessity to labor. They felt that the world owed them a living which was withheld by the white people and dealt out only as they could work or cajole it out of them. But Tuskegee, Hampton, and the scores of offshoot schools which have trained tradesmen and emphasized character have made a real impression on this attitude toward work.

The other set of forces which tends to elevate the standard of Negro labor comes from the white employer class. At a time when the greatest need of the South is for labor to till its idle fields and develop its infant industries, loafing becomes almost criminal. Foremen become more expert in weeding out the floaters and gradually the man who likes to work three days and rest four, finds it harder and harder to get back on the pay roll, and the number of sober, industrious, unskilled laborers increases. Upon these sober, industrious black laborers, the Southern towns depend, almost wholly, for the performance of the heavy work which is necessary for their prosperity.

Manufacturing is gaining more prominence in Southern economic life. Forward-looking leaders are beginning to see that a perfectly balanced prosperity will depend upon the development of Southern industry so that there will be a more equal adjustment between the country and the city populations. To attain this the South must offer attractions to capital. In natural resources the section is rich. The timber, clays, marls, limestones, granite, marble, coal, ores, and water power make the South one of nature's veritable treasure houses. In labor the South is potentially rich. The war experience has proved what can be done to raise the standards of colored labor when the task is approached with intelligence and sympathy. But, in addition to the natural resources and the potential labor supply, capital must be attracted from the outside; and to attract outside capital the South must convince the industrialists of other sections that it offers great opportunities.

The efficiency of the South's great labor supply will be fully as potent a factor in attracting capital as the richness of natural resources. To develop it, the South must do two things. First: every means must be used to increase the capacity of the individual, Negro and white, through education and encouragement. Second: those community conditions which are driving the Negroes away to other sections must be corrected. In other words the industrial future of the South is conditioned on better educational facilities, more adequate protection, better health, and more even-handed justice for the Negro. The South must appeal to the Negro laborer as a land of industrial opportunity.

SKILLED LABOR

The development of industry and the progress of the colored people does not, however, depend so much upon the masses of common labor as it does upon the growing number of skilled artisans and mechanics. Without this group of higher paid workmen as a stimulating example, and as a group furnishing leadership, the common laborer would feel that there is no hope for his progress or for the advancement of his children, and the benumbing clouds of hopelessness would settle around him and render his labor a heartless and grudging service. The table on the following page indicates the lines in which the largest numbers of Negroes have risen.

There were substantial and even rapid increases in the industrial trades, especially in foremen, machinists, metal molders, and pourers. It is notable, however, that, even in a period of great demand for labor, there were substantial decreases in several hand trades, including masons, blacksmiths, dressmakers, and seamstresses (outside of factories). This is due largely to the increased competition from white skilled workers in the South.

One of the economic tendencies which alarmed Booker T. Washington about 1890, and which tinged all his speeches and writings on industrial education, was the increasing competition and encroachment by the white man in several lines of skilled labor and business which, immediately after the Civil War, were practically monopolized by Negroes.

NEGROES IN TRADES AND PROFESSIONS

	1920	1910
Teachers	36,626	29,674
Preachers	19,571	17,495
Physicians and surgeons	3,495	3,077
Dentists	1,109	478
Trained nurses	3,341	2,433
Total professions	64,142	53,157
Carpenters	34,243	30,468
Dressmakers and seamstresses (not in factory)	26,973	38,216
Machinists and toolmakers	10,286	3,323
Other mechanics	8,990	752
Masons	10,609	12,403
Painters	9,432	8,927
Blacksmiths	8,886	9,837
Plasterers	7,082	6,175
Tailor and tailoress	6,893	5,043
Metal molders, pourers, etc.	6,634	2,221
Engineers (other than locomotive)	6,353	4,857
Shoemakers (not in factories)	4,707	3,739
Foremen (industrial and mining)	3,885	1,796
Plumbers	3,516	2,285
Furnace men, smelter men, etc.	3,236	3,206
Bakers	3,164	2,125
Printing trades	1,719	1,318
Filers, grinders, polishers, etc.	1,618	441
Electricians	1,342	703
Builders and contractors	1,454	3,293

Using this as a warning, he urged industrial education, strict attention to duty, efficiency, and thrift as the only salvation of colored skilled workers. Between 1890 and 1900 the Negro actually lost ground in such important trades as carpentry, plastering, and blacksmithing. Race prejudice, difficulties with trades unions, increasing numbers of white skilled workers, and, in some cases, lack of proper application and efficiency on the part of the colored workers themselves, militated against them.

The effectiveness of the propaganda of Washington and his school of leaders is shown, however, by the fact that this tendency was arrested about 1900 and the 1910 census showed these skilled tradesmen increasing in numbers. The 1920 census again shows substantial gains in colored carpenters, plasterers, painters, and plumbers, as against losses only in blacksmithing and masonry. The sons of the men whose skill fashioned the stately buildings of the old South evidently have a fine opportunity to continue in the building trades if they render a high grade of service, and in addition new opportunities to enter the factory trades have been offered.

The skill and stamina of colored workers in other lines than the building trades is attested by their conduct under the pressure which the emergencies of national defense placed upon war-time workers. Records in two important operations were broken by Negroes. Edward Burwell, the Negro pile-driving captain, with a crew of eleven, broke the world's record by driving 220 sixty-five-foot piles in nine hours and five minutes. Most of the work was done in a steady downpour of rain and the log of his crew shows several mechanical difficulties which slowed them down during the day, but these were overcome and the work attacked with renewed vigor. His record was fifty-five piles ahead of the previous record. In the plant of the Bethlehem Steel Corporation at Sparrow's Point, a Negro crew broke the record for driving rivets. One of the gang, Charles Knight, drove 4875 three-quarter-inch rivets in a nine-hour day. Such work is manifestly a very valuable asset to industry and the work of thousands of others who did not attain such publicity but who, nevertheless, measured up to the standard of a full day's work, well done, is of great economic value.

But the Negro skilled worker faces many difficulties in earning a living. The chief of these arise from race prejudice. The wages paid the colored worker are often lower than those paid the white worker for the same service. On piecework he is often assigned the more difficult patterns with the result that his output is smaller. In trades where some processes are higher paid than others (such as rough- and smooth-stone masonry) he sometimes cannot gain access to those which pay better. All investigations of the position of the Negro in industry show that there is a wide difference in policy as to the payment of equal wages, employment for equal hours, and employment in similar processes. The Negro's treatment in these respects is largely dependent upon the sense of justice of individual employers.

The Negro and Organized Labor

Many of the difficulties of Negro workers arise from their relation to the labor organizations. But the report of the Chicago commission points out "There is a gradually increasing sympathetic understanding by unionists of the struggle of Negroes to overcome their handicaps, and an increasing realization of the importance to the union of organizing them. Negroes are, themselves, showing more interest in efforts toward organization, but there is still much mutual suspicion and resentment in their relations." Of the 116 national and international unions studied in Chicago, 104 admit Negroes and 12 do not.

In the past the trouble has been largely because of the attitude of local unions. Though the American Federation and many national and international labor bodies have declared policies of non-discrimination, the local unions have been autonomous and have often excluded Negroes. This exclusion from local unions has applied especially in the North. In the South, where Negroes have always formed such a large proportion of the labor supply, unions, when organized, have usually included Negro and white workers in separate, coöperating locals.

Exclusion from the union has often forced the Negro into the position of a strike breaker. When he has been denied admission a strike presents the first opportunity to the Negro to enter that line of work. The ensuing clashes, occurring in the superheated atmosphere of a strike, have left bitterness and misunderstanding on both sides. The Chicago stockyards strike of 1904 was broken by Negroes and the investigation of the commission on race relations, almost twenty years afterward, revealed lingering traces of the bitterness which arose during that strike. Of the many examples of this kind the steel strike of 1920 was probably the largest.

Labor unions have been forced to organize Negroes because it has been impossible for them to ignore this great mass of laborers, who, if unorganized, would defeat their program. As was the case with immigrant foreigners, this recognition has been tardy, and its tardiness has aroused suspicions as to the genuineness of the program of organized labor.

At present, however, there are three ways in which the unions deal with colored labor:

1. Organization in separate subordinate locals.
2. Organization in separate coördinate locals.
3. Inclusion in the same local with white laborers.

The efforts to include them in separate subordinate locals, where white grievance committees handle all their grievances, are not successful, and only a few locals follow this policy. The Negroes are suspicious of such efforts. The organization of separate coördinate locals is undertaken in some cases because of the preference of the colored workers themselves, and sometimes because of unwillingness of white workers to admit Negroes. In either case, when the locals are truly coördinate, and where they coöperate in all matters through fair representation on district councils, the colored workers seem satisfied with the results obtained. When organized in the same local union the relationships seem to be entirely satisfactory unless the local attempts some social function in addition to its business transaction.

This adjustment of the Negro and organized labor is one of the most important phases of race relations because some of the most violent friction arises from economic contacts, especially during periods of unemployment. In such periods the Negro at work is the target of the jealousy of the white man out of work, and the idle Negro is the scapegoat for crime in the community. Many employers follow the just policy of laying men off according to seniority, regardless of color. But the white man thrown out of work in this way often feels resentment toward the Negro retained, even though the colored man had been working for the plant a long time. On the other hand some employers, when slack times come, lay off all their Negroes first, regardless of seniority. This creates a deep resentment and feeling of injustice among the Negroes.

Unemployment, with the resultant friction and bitterness, was one of the major factors in the riots of East St. Louis, Coatesville, Springfield, and Chicago. Such serious results are to be guarded against at all costs, and one safeguard is for the employer and the white laborer to recognize the justice of retaining men on the basis of their length of service in a plant, whether they are white or colored.

Negro or Foreigner?

The situation which confronts the United States is briefly this : Industry periodically exerts a brisk demand for labor. Formerly this labor was plentifully supplied by immigration from Europe, but more recently, when immigration was cut off, first by war and later by congressional legislation, industry drew on the farms of America for white and colored labor. This raises the question as to whether the country's need for labor is to be supplied by lowering the immigration bars again or by increasing the efficiency of the individual laborers now in the United States.

The migration of the Negro from Southern farms has made many Southern Democrats feel that possibly European immigration should be encouraged to alleviate this situation. The movement of Negroes from Southern farms is, however, no more serious than the movement of native American boys and girls from the farms of New England and the

Middle West. This is a question of broad national significance and one which is too fundamental to be decided on the basis of racial or sectional feeling.

There can be no doubt that the Negroes have been in America so many generations that they are more American in their ideals and adherence to American institutions than is generally realized. In the first place they speak the language, and any manufacturer who has had to employ interpreters to issue orders to his foreign laborers will attest the value of English-speaking labor. Again the Negro has more of the American attitude of employee to boss than has the European, especially the Slav, immigrant. Thus in many ways the Negro is an American laborer and a real asset to American industry, if only efforts are directed toward developing his good qualities. Talks with a number of manufacturers will convince the skeptic that, compared with the non-English-speaking foreigner, the Negro is the more valuable asset to industry. The full development of the capabilities of the five million Negro laborers will, in a great measure, aid the country to develop its agriculture and industry without the strain on American ideals and institutions which is imposed by the effort to assimilate hundreds of thousands of immigrants of different cultures, many of whom come only to accumulate a little money and then return to their native land and never have any attachment to, or abiding interest in, the United States.

CONSTRUCTIVE LABOR POLICY

There is, however, a great need for more knowledge and a more sympathetic understanding between agricultural and industrial leaders as a basis of a labor policy which will allow industry to expand normally without crippling the farmer. As it operates at present, industry is taking thousands of laborers from the farm, and this process is going on faster than the farmer can adjust himself to it by more intensive cultivation and use of machinery. All agencies, both national and state, should therefore devote particular attention to this balance of agricultural and industrial labor, especially as it applies to Negro labor.

A good beginning along this line was made by the federal government during the war when it installed a Bureau of Negro Economics in the United States Department of Labor, and placed at its head a scholarly and competent colored man. This policy did not, however, continue more than a year or two before this man was replaced by a typical Negro politician with no training and no real interest in the laboring conditions of his people.

The action of state departments of labor has been almost entirely confined to Southern states, where it has been limited to the administration of laws directed against the operation of labor agents. These laws have required an excessive license fee from each man shipping labor outside the state. Such action is repressive and extremely short-sighted. It is designed to interfere with the free movement of labor and, in the long run, it reacts against industry within the South. Construction companies in the South desiring labor to carry on their work are often seriously hampered by this restriction against recruiting their men in neighboring states. The northward migration is hardly affected by these laws, since Negroes continue to go whether solicited by labor agents or not. Such laws also make it extremely difficult to operate employment bureaus in

Southern cities where such bureaus would be most valuable in placing colored labor.

An agency in the Eastern and Middle Western industrial districts which is proving valuable in adjusting the Negro to industry is the National Urban League. This organization operates employment bureaus in a number of industrial centers and places thousands of colored workmen. In addition they study working conditions carefully and endeavor to improve them. They also deliver shop talks to the workmen and endeavor to raise their efficiency. They are constantly on the lookout for new lines of work into which Negroes may enter and prove their usefulness.

The United States Department of Labor could render signal service in this field by extending its free employment service to colored people as rapidly as possible. In 1923 almost a million and a half job seekers were placed by the government offices. Only a few branches, however, handle colored applications. This leaves the jobless colored man dependent upon his own devices or upon the commercial employment agencies, many of which charge exorbitant rates. In periods when Negro laborers are shifting so rapidly from country to city such bureaus are greatly needed as aids for fitting the rural Negro into the economic life of the city.

The task of adjusting the colored labor supply to American industry, of striking a balance between Southern agriculture and Northern industry, and of determining the relation of the Negro to the immigrant, to the union, and to the industrial community is one of so many complications and such vast scope that it demands the full and intelligent coöperation of all agencies, — federal, state, and private.

The Negro in Business

In business, the Negro has also made most creditable advances. Slavery was not a training calculated to inculcate the thrift, foresight, and executive ability necessary for business success. Yet, soon after emancipation, numbers of small Negro business enterprises were launched. They were mainly barber shops, catering establishments, and restaurants.

These early businesses catering to white trade have, however, almost entirely disappeared. White people entered the same lines of business, and drove most of their small Negro competitors out by the application of superior managerial ability and more capital. Prejudice against patronizing Negroes also played its part. Many of the Negro proprietors continued in business catering to the trade of Negroes instead of the trade of white people, but many were driven into other lines. Gone are the famous Negro caterers and restaurateurs of the former generation. They have been compelled either to operate restaurants for their own people or to accept positions as waiters. Most of the famous old barber shops have also been replaced by white barbers, and, with only a few exceptions, Negro barber shops are for Negro patronage.

A new type of Negro business has, however, replaced the old. Negroes now have their own banks, insurance companies, newspapers, and real estate agents. Prejudice, while operating against the old type of business, has operated in favor of the new. Refusal of old line life insurance companies to insure Negroes has led to the establishment of separate Negro companies. Discourtesies and inconveniences in banks and retail houses have led to the establishment of these businesses by Negroes for Negroes.

One of the most prominent colored business men of the country tells of the time when he entered the largest shoe store in his town to purchase shoes. When he had selected his style the clerk wrapped up the pair of shoes and handed them to him. He said, of course, that he would like to try them on to see whether or not they fitted, before taking them. He was informed, however, that that store did not try on shoes for Negroes. On passing out of the store he observed, across the way, the bank in which that store kept its money and in which he had quite a large account. He immediately resolved that his people should have a bank so that their financial power could be mobilized and they could develop retail businesses of their own.

The census of 1920 indicates the following distribution of principal Negro businesses :

BUSINESS	NUMBER OF ESTABLISHMENTS
Hotel keepers and managers	1,020
Restaurant and lunch room	7,511
Barbers	2,500
Hairdressers and manicures and toilet goods	3,500
Shoemakers (not in factories)	2,700
Retailers	23,526
Bankers, brokers, and money lenders	142
Undertakers	1,558
Real estate	500
Theatrical proprietors	185
Tailoring	4,000
Laundry proprietors	199
Insurance	173
Total	40,686

Retailers, restaurateurs, barbers, tailors, shoemakers, and undertakers are still the most numerous. Their success is all the more notable because it has been won in spite of the fact that they have been compelled to operate with the assistance of employees chosen from a people untrained in business, and they have been compelled to deal with customers of the same type. They do not have the organized credit facilities and coöperative association which are available to the white business man.

In point of numbers the banks, insurance companies, and real estate offices are few, but their significance in the Negro business world is great both because of the amount of money they have been able to accumulate and because of the service which they are in a position to render their people.

The mortality among Negroes was so high immediately after emancipation that the larger insurance companies refused all Negroes as risks, and many of them did not even accept Negroes for industrial insurance. As a result Negro secret orders sprang up, which in nearly every instance emphasized the sick benefit and industrial insurance feature. These lodges were the training ground for Negroes in insurance, and later separate insurance companies were developed. The Negro Year Book lists sixty insurance companies, aside from the fraternal orders. These companies have assets of about $6,500,000, with an annual income of about $9,000,000, and a total insurance in force of about $100,000,000. The accumulation of this great sum of money not only provides security for the thousands of small policy holders in these companies, but also swells bank deposits and provides capital for mortgages and conservative real estate investments.

The masses of colored people are thoroughly converted to insurance. In fact, among the lower classes too much "sickness and burial" insurance is carried. It is not at all unusual to find a poor widow who subsists on hand laundry, carrying four or five of these "ten cent a week" policies.

The history of Negro banking is filled with tragic failures and yet there are a number of strong, well-established colored banks which are serving the race. In 1922 there were 74 Negro banks with combined resources of about $20,000,000. Some of the failures of the past have been due to the fact that colored banks, in times of stringency, do not have the reserves to fall back upon which are available to white banks. There has, however, been a recent tendency upon the part of white banks to be more liberal in aiding colored banks to tide over their periods of stress, provided they have been organized and operated along sound lines.

Real estate is another field which offers profit and a chance for genuine service to the colored business man. The housing conditions for colored people are so poor, and profiteering in high rents so universal, that the man who opens subdivisions for colored people and sells at a reasonable profit makes money, and at the same time serves a real community need. Up to date, the colored owners of real estate have, however, imitated their white contemporaries by charging their own people all that the market would bear. A few instances of public-spirited real estate men are, however, to be found. The most notable of these have been the Service Realty Company of Atlanta and Augusta, Georgia; The Schmidlapp Foundation of Cincinnati, Ohio; and the Titustown Development Company of Norfolk, Virginia. These companies have purchased and developed large tracts. Neat homes with space around them and attractively laid out yards have been sold on easy terms to colored people. They have usually made comfortable profits and at the same time have rendered a genuine service in relieving the congestion of the colored sections.

As colored business men develop, a new factor is injected into colored leadership. The business man is more in touch with the economic life of his people and is usually more practical than the teacher or the preacher. He thus provides a balance wheel for the colored community and develops practical methods of encouraging thrift and economic independence.

The National Negro Business League, organized by Booker T. Washington, with local branches all over the country, is doing much to give these business men a morale, and to provide opportunities for them to profit by their colleagues' experiences and to work out methods of coöperation.

There are, therefore, many reasons for encouraging the Negro business men. They not only constitute a conservative and valuable leadership group, but they also encourage their people in thrift. Their operations create clerical employment for thousands of young colored men and women.

BIBLIOGRAPHY

EPSTEIN, A. The Negroes of Pittsburgh.

Harrison and Associates, Russell Sage Foundation, Public Employment offices, pp. 605–610.

HART, A. B. The Southern South, Chapter X.

HAYNES, GEORGE. The Negro at Work in New York City.

MURPHY, E. G. The Present South, pp. 78–85.

OVINGTON, M. W. Half a Man, pp. 95–105.

Report of the Chicago Commission on Race Relations, "The Negro in Chicago," Chapter VIII.

United States Department of Labor. "Negro Migration, 1916–1917," pp. 129–138.

United States Department of Labor. "The Negro at Work during the War and Reconstruction."

WASHINGTON, B. T. The Negro in Business.

WASHINGTON, B. T. The Story of the Negro, Chapter III.

TOPICS FOR STUDY AND DISCUSSION

1. From the economic standpoint what occupations engage the "upper tenth" of the Negro population?

2. What occupational opportunities cause an excess of females in certain cities and of males in others? (List twenty cities from the census and study sex and age distribution of the Negro population.)

3. From Department of Labor Bulletin ("The Negro at Work during the World War and Reconstruction"), from the Chicago Report, and by observation of conditions in a particular community, determine the extent to which Negroes receive lower pay than white people for the same type of work.

4. Discuss the burden which domestic service places upon the community in day nursery problems, orphanage problems, and problems of juvenile delinquency.

5. Study the table of occupations in 1910 and 1920. Is the drift toward the mechanical or non-mechanical trades? What light does this throw on the former belief that Negroes could not be trained to handle machinery?

6. Discuss the relationship of the Negro to trade unions. In what way has prejudice led the unions to injure their own cause?

7. Outline a constructive policy for dealing with Negro labor, by the labor organizations, by the federal government, by state governments, and by local communities.

8. What is the effect of race prejudice on the growth of Negro business?

9. What is the effect of the industrial movement on living conditions of Negroes?

CHAPTER VII

LAW AND ORDER

In the successful adjustment of the legal relationships of the two races democracy is vitally involved. The right to a fair trial by an impartial jury of peers is one of the bedrocks upon which freedom rests, and if it cannot be preserved when the courts serve two races, then democracy itself rests on quicksand. The problem of legal justice is, therefore, fully as important to the white race as to the Negro race. Any tendency to weaken the feeling that the court system is entirely impartial, unaffected by passion or prejudice, and meticulously just, or any tendency to strengthen the feeling that the court can be biased or made the instrument of a particular class, is a tendency which may wreck society. Like the machinery of government, the machinery of justice is entirely in the hands of the white man. He makes the laws which courts enforce, he has evolved the court system, he furnishes the judges, court officers, and juries. It is therefore his great responsibility, in face of any difficulty, to render justice through them.

The descendants of the Anglo-Saxon have gained a supremacy in many lands because they have been supremely fair and supremely just. A departure from fair and just policies will inevitably sap their moral stamina and endanger their hard-won supremacy, for supremacy is not an individual or a racial heritage. It must be constantly maintained.

NEGRO CRIME RATE

The necessity of dealing with a large number of backward colored people puts a strain upon the courts. The pressure of prejudice and jealousy, and the desire by some classes of white people to exploit, often leads to injustice toward the Negro. On the other hand, the presence of large numbers of Negroes, as yet poorly adapted to the codes and institutions of the white civilization in which they live, brings problems of law and morals to both races. The task of preserving law and order is therefore twofold, consisting of efforts to reduce the crime among the irresponsible class of Negroes, and to reduce the violence and injustice among the irresponsible class of white people. In fact, the Negro race has a large, but not excessive, criminal element, but, with the exception of thefts, the great majority of his crimes are committed against other Negroes. A study of the crime rate indicates that their criminality is not attributable to racial tendencies so much as it is to living conditions.

The following figures indicate the extent and something of the distribution of Negro criminality.

PRISONERS AND JUVENILE DELINQUENTS: COMMITMENT
RATES PER 100,000 OF EACH RACE, 1910

	WHITE	NEGRO
Total	467	1,102
The South	258	880
The North	503	2,836
The West	816	3,667

Thus one out of every hundred Negroes and one of every two hundred and fifty whites were committed to prison in 1910. The rate for Negroes is more than twice the rate for white people, but one out of each hundred is not a sufficiently large proportion to warrant branding the race as having deep-rooted criminal tendencies.

In passing, it may be said that the Negro crime rate appears higher than the actual amount of criminality because of injustices in the courts. It is a notorious fact that in many sections the Negro who becomes involved in the toils of the law can gain his freedom only by a stroke of fortune or by extraordinary effort. The arrest and conviction of innocent Negroes, therefore, swells the commitment rate beyond the actual volume of crime.

Causes of Crime

The variations in the different sections furnish further clews as to the real reasons for Negro crime. The South, with a large rural population which has become adapted to its situation, has a low crime rate for both white people and Negroes. The North and West, where the Negro population is largely concentrated in cities and where it has recently migrated, have Negro crime rates three and a half and four and a half times as high as the South. In the West North-Central section, which approaches the South in its proportion of rural inhabitants, the commitment rate for native white people was only 296 per hundred thousand, but the commitment rate for foreign-born whites was 550. That is, among the migrant whites the crime rate was twice that of the natives. These rates of crime among the native and foreign born are comparable to those of the white and colored people in the South. This influence of city life and migration on the crime rate is further evident from the rates in New England with 630 commitments per 100,000 native whites and 1143 for the same number of foreign born. In other words, the crime rate among the foreign born in New England is higher than the crime rate among the Negroes in the United States.

Another factor in the crime rate is the inadequate care of the insane and the feeble-minded. Many of these are not confined in institutions. This is especially true of the feeble-minded, there being no institution for the segregation of the colored cases in the Southern states. A study of the inmates of the Georgia penitentiary showed that 60 per cent of the Negro inmates were feeble-minded. From this it is evident that a proper understanding and care of this element of the population would greatly reduce crime.

The outstanding causes of Negro criminality may, therefore, be said to be : The Negro's racial background, *i.e.*, his lack of adaptation to the codes and institutions of the white race; his migration from country to city; the adverse economic and housing conditions surrounding him; and feeble-mindedness. Only the last of these is due to inborn traits. The others can be minimized by education, painstaking effort to adjust the Negro to American life, and humane and modern administration of penal institutions.

Lack of modern, humane methods of dealing with Negro offenders hampers many sections in reducing crime. All phases of contact between society and the criminal or suspect need to be thoroughly safeguarded. Extreme care should be taken in making arrests. Those committed to jails, penitentiaries, or reformatories should be surrounded, in these institutions, with conditions which will tend to correct their criminal tendencies rather than with conditions which tend to debase, brutalize, and increase criminal tendencies. Every effort should be made to return them to society as useful citizens. Adequate institutional treatment should also be supplemented with modern systems of probation and parole.

LENGTH OF SENTENCE

In the North and in the South virtually the same proportion of Negroes are committed for minor offenses, yet there is a striking inequality in the length of sentences served. The proportion of long sentences in the South is unduly high :

PER CENT COMMITTED (1910) FOR

	OVER ONE YEAR	ONE MONTH TO ONE YEAR	ONE MONTH OR LESS
White commitments			
North	6.9	53.9	39.2
South	33.8	37.8	28.4
Negro commitments			
North	16.0	53.5	30.5
South	42.3	40.4	17.4

Thus almost a half of the Negroes in the South are committed for a year or more, while only about a sixth of the Northern Negroes are given such a long term ; and only a sixth of the Southern Negroes are committed for one month or less while a third of the Northern commitments are for this short period. The fact that the commitments are also longer for white people in the South indicates that some of this discrepancy in length of sentence is due to a sectional rather than a racial difference in administration of justice. The purely sectional tendency to impose longer sentences in the South on both races does not, however, fully account for the great proportion of Southern Negroes committed for over a year and the very small proportion committed for less than a month.

It indicates a definite tendency on the part of Southern courts to impose heavier sentences on the Negro than upon white men, and heavier sentences than those imposed by the Northern courts. The strikingly small number of commitments for less than a month is also indicative of a tendency on the part of Southern judges to condone or merely reprimand certain peccadillos of the Negro which are punished with short imprisonment in the North. In some sections, the system of employing convicts on the roads of the county in which they are convicted influences court officials and judges to impose heavy sentences, but in most instances there is an honest belief on the part of the judge that the best way to correct the Negro is to follow the method applied to children and either merely reprimand and warn, or impose a heavy punishment.

UNJUST ARREST

One of the most persistent complaints of Negroes, North and South, arises from the conduct of arresting officers. No adequate figures as to arrests are available, but if they could be secured, the number of useless arrests of Negroes would prove astounding. The fee system, which allows officers a fee for each arrest and allots to judges, solicitors, and sheriffs a proportion of the court costs of trials, is a vicious factor in this useless arrest.

The following quotation from a leading Georgia daily during the migration indicates that some of the Southern communities are waking up to this consideration :

Everybody seems to be asleep about what is going on right under our noses, — that is, everybody but those farmers who waked up on mornings recently to find every Negro over twenty-one on their places gone. . . .

And we go about our affairs as usual — our police raid pool rooms for "loafing Negroes," bring in twelve, and keep them in the barracks all night, and next morning find that ten of them have steady jobs and were merely there to spend an hour in the only indoor recreation they have; our county officers hear of a disturbance at a Negro resort and bring in fifty-odd men, women, boys, and girls to spend the night in jail, to make a bond at 10 per cent, to hire lawyers, to mortgage half of two months' pay to get back to their jobs Monday morning, although but half a dozen of them could have been guilty of disorderly conduct.

A Mississippi daily adds the following:

We allow petty officers of the law to harass and oppress our Negro labor, mulcting them of their wages, assessing stiff fines on trivial charges, and often they are convicted on charges, which if preferred against a white man, would result in prompt acquittal.

Nor are these practices confined to the South. The following record of events is traceable in the files of the daily papers of a large Northern city which has recently received a considerable influx of Negro migrants. There was a period of industrial unemployment attended, as usual, by a series of thefts and holdups. The chief of police was roundly criticized by the "out" faction for not bringing the thieves to justice. He blamed the large number of Negro unemployed for the situation, and announced that on a certain Friday night he would conduct a clean-up of the Negro ward. As this announcement was printed on Wednesday it is extremely improbable that any criminal remained in that ward to wait for his raid on Friday, nevertheless it was conducted. Every Negro pool room was entered and 160 arrests were made. All but 20 of these were charged with the technical offense of vagrancy. Of the 140 vagrants about 60 were finally able to show enough money or sufficient employment to clear themselves from that charge. The other 80 were convicted of vagrancy and released on condition that they leave town immediately. One of these who had no money tried to walk out of town but was re-arrested and brought back twice; then he tried stealing out on freight trains and was brought back by railroad detectives twice, until the judge, in desperation, had one of the bailiffs take him in his own car to the city limits. In remarking on this, the leading daily said that with such brilliant activity on the part of the police department, it was a mystery why the thievery and hold-ups continued unabated.

This high-handed arrest of colored people is extremely galling to the law-abiding citizens, who often live constantly in fear that they, at any time, may be causelessly subjected to this humiliation. It cannot be excused on any ground other than ignorance and inefficiency of police officers who engage in these practices, and indifference of the citizens who permit such officers to remain on the job.

REFORMATION

As a rule the faults of jails, chain gangs, and penitentiaries apply to white and colored alike except that in many jails, where the two races are segregated, the Negroes have the more unsanitary quarters. Mr. G. Croft Williams of the South Carolina Board of Welfare observes that "the average jail is not an exhibition of the citizenry's cruelty, but of their callous neglect. All professions of humanitarianism and of the sincere desire to make a better and happier world will echo back in hollow mockery as long as our present jails stand as their sounding boards."

It is not the province of this book to go into the horrors of the jails, chain gangs and road camps of some states. Experts have painted terrible pictures and reports of official investigating committees contain authoritative statements as to the exposure, the debasement, the filth, and the inhumanity of the surroundings of criminals placed in some convict camps. It must be realized that the society which places a white man or a black man in such an environment for several months can expect nothing else than that he return to society more debased and more inclined to crime.

It is only very recently that the need for special treatment for juvenile delinquents has been widely understood, and the task of caring for the white juvenile delinquent is much further advanced than that of caring for the colored. In many instances ignorance of the law, lack of the proper place of detention or of the proper machinery for probation leads to placing juvenile delinquents in jail alongside of hardened criminals. This is not corrective but debasing. It does not lessen criminality but brings recruits to the criminal ranks.

Most of the Southern states have some kind of reformatory for colored boys, but only Virginia, Kentucky, Oklahoma, Tennessee, and South Carolina provide such an institution for colored girls. A movement is on foot in several other states to make provision to meet this need. Without such an institution many judges are unwilling to place colored girls who have committed minor offenses in jail. They merely release them to go back into their vicious environment, drift into worse habits and finally to become criminals. In the larger counties this is a serious situation.

If probation officers are white, they have great difficulty in gaining the confidence of the Negro probationers. The barrier of color is between them and their charge. A few large counties have found the solution of this situation in the employment of colored probation officers. The first colored probation officer was employed only as late as 1915, but since that time several large counties have added such workers to their staff and found that the service which they render in correcting colored boys and girls is invaluable to the community. There is a great need for the extension of this work, and counties whose revenues do not warrant the employment of a full-time officer are in need of part-time or voluntary probation service for colored delinquents. The Negroes themselves need to take a more enlightened and active interest in this great problem of theirs, and to manifest this interest by organizing juvenile delinquency councils which will coöperate with the juvenile courts in handling the colored cases.

With these adverse influences in living conditions, feeble-mindedness, unjust arrests, penal institutions and probation, the marvel is, not that one in each hundred Negroes is a convicted criminal, but that the rate is as low as it is.

INJUSTICES IN THE COURTS

The injustices to which the courts subject the Negro are largely the product of three things : prejudice, the economic condition of the Negro who is involved in court, and the unreliability of the testimony of many Negroes. Not only

is this true in criminal cases, but it also applies to civil suits
in which a Negro is involved with a white man. Wherever a
Negro is arrayed against a white man it is the old story of
the weak against the strong. The report of the Carnegie
Foundation on "Justice and the Poor" showed vividly that
the poor man, whether he is white or black, is at a grave
disadvantage when he attempts to secure justice in the
courts. Studies of the relation of the immigrant to the court
show that he suffers many of the same disadvantages as the
Negro. Lawyers, not clients, secure justice, and the man
who can employ competent counsel, and who has friends
among the court officials and jurymen, has all the advantage
on his side.

Legal aid, when wisely administered, can do much to
adjust this balance. There are now a few legal aid agencies
in the South but, for the most part, the legal aid which
Negroes receive is informal and unorganized. If the Negro
who gets in trouble has a kind-hearted employer, or white
friend who will secure a good lawyer for him, and will aid in
getting witnesses to testify, he has an excellent chance to get
justice, often to get more than justice. If, on the other
hand, he is friendless, the small fee which he is able to pay
often limits him to the services of a young, inexperienced, or
an older shyster lawyer. The practices indulged in by some
of these men who make a habit of soliciting Negro business
around the jail is a disgrace to the legal profession and
should subject them to disbarment. A well-organized legal
aid society which would take only those cases which were
thoroughly investigated beforehand, would divert much of
the business from these less able lawyers and correct many
of the injustices suffered by the Negro.

Again, there is much honest doubt in the minds of those who are experienced in handling Negro testimony as to when to believe and when not to believe this testimony in court. This is not due so much to any racial difference in attitude toward truth as it is to difference in mental attributes. The masses of Negroes are ignorant and highly excitable. Such people, in reporting events, often report their feelings rather than what they actually see and hear. They feel the events so keenly that they obtain a distorted notion of what is happening and actually believe that what they relate is true; but they can easily be tripped up and discredited before a jury by an experienced cross examiner. This has occurred so habitually that many jurymen flatly refuse to believe Negro testimony, and this condition will continue until training and self-control render the statements of the masses of Negroes more reliable, even when made under emotional stress. This condition makes possible the rise of the loan-shark evil, exploitation by merchants and landlords, and peonage, against which the friendless Negro has little chance of redress in the courts unless he is extended legal aid.

LYNCHING

Lynching is the most spectacular and intensified injustice to the Negro. It is the one which agitates both the leaders and the masses most profoundly. At the same time it constitutes the greatest menace to white civilization. In the heat of a debate on international policies and in the midst of the controversies of a presidential campaign, Congress passed a resolution deploring the "British atrocities in Ireland." The Canadian Parliament immediately retaliated with a resolution condemning mob violence in the United States. This was merely a piece of mutual legislative impertinence, but the response of the Canadians is a matter for careful thought. The potential influence of such ideals as the United States may sponsor is seriously challenged when Canadian Members of Parliament, Japanese publicists, and Tagore and his Indian followers inquire whether promiscuous hanging and burning of fellow human beings are symbols of American civilization and democracy, when the prominent European journals feature the vilest actions of the mob, and when the people of Haiti and Mexico say that they see no reason why mob control of their countries gives us the excuse for intervention in their affairs when our own mobs are so violent and go unpunished.

From these angles it is evident that lynching is a matter of more than nation-wide importance. Indeed it has assumed international aspects. Mob violence seems to be confined largely to America, but it is not confined to the Southern states. There the mob lynches; elsewhere it indulges in strike riots, race riots, or gang killings and bombings. These are diabolical blots on American civilization. A description of the barbarous details of lynchings would be too revolting to print, but the investigator of these cases could parallel the inhuman horrors of the Spanish inquisition in the action of mobs in twentieth-century America.

The most conservative records of mob actions list some four thousand victims of lynchers alone since 1885. In other words, during the past thirty-eight years Judge Lynch has executed on the average of two victims per week. This includes only persons who were accused or suspected of some crime. If a similar record could be compiled of the victims of race riots and strike mobs, the total would probably reach ten thousand. Judge Lynch has been active long enough to be an institution in some communities. He is a part of the hardened cake of custom and will not be easily dislodged. There are, however, methods by which his hold can be weakened. The facts indicate that they are the long slow methods of community education and local action rather than some sudden reform by the passage of an act of Congress. A deep-rooted custom has never been legislated out of existence in a hurry.

One of the excuses of those who apologize for lynching is that it avenges a particular brutal and abhorrent crime which would be given too much publicity by court action. An examination of the facts does not bear out this statement. The majority of the lynchings are not for rape but for violence. The causes are as follows:

Murder and assault, 43.6 per cent; rape or attempted rape, 23.0; theft, 7.4; other causes, 26.0. Thus while the mob may begin by lynching for one crime, once their blood lust is aroused they lynch for other crimes and sometimes for fancied offenses. As to publicity there is no comparison between the notice given an orderly court trial and that accorded by the flaming headlines which greet a lynching. In this respect the mob defeats its avowed purpose of protecting an innocent victim from the focus of public attention.

COMBATING THE MOB

On the face of the record it is evident that mob rule is a temporary but vicious manifestation of a spirit of anarchy, and is, to an alarming degree, unpunished. In view of this condition it is regrettable that the present constitution and machinery of the federal government seem unable to do anything effective to check this great evil. An attempt was made through the Dyer bill, which was introduced and shelved in the 1922 session of Congress and reintroduced in 1924. The intent of this bill was to make participation in a mob an offense which may be punished by federal courts. The bill also provided that a fine of $10,000 be assessed against any county in which mob violence was committed and provided penalties against negligent public officials.

Nothing was ever rationally settled by partisan or sectional controversy, and when the debate becomes both partisan and sectional, the result is disastrously unsettling. In handling the Dyer anti-lynching bill, Congress developed little but partisan and sectional arguments. The net result was that the national attitude toward this question of fundamental importance has been decidedly muddled. Northern Congressmen tore their hair over the lynching record of the Southern states, — and it is black enough. But Southern Congressmen merely countered with citations of the race and strike riots of Northern cities. In addition there were honest doubts on both sides as to whether or not it is constitutional to take this particular form of crime, now in the hands of the state courts, and place it in the jurisdiction of the federal courts.

Aside from the constitutionality of federal interference in lynching, the fundamental objection to this course, which was hardly touched on in Congress, is that the federal courts would, in all probability, be less effective than state courts, and the act of giving the federal courts and officials responsibility would lessen the very essential sense of responsibility now developing among state and county officials. Many local sheriffs and police officers would shrug their shoulders and say: "Now that Uncle Sam has taken hold, that lets me out. The United States marshal is welcome to the job."

To those who have watched the federal courts in their efforts to enforce the prohibition law, it is evident that much is to be said in favor of leaving the power and the responsibility in the hands of local officials. In some of the states which had prohibition laws before the passage of the federal act, the flagrant violations of the national law have led to the belief that the previous state enforcement was more effective than the present federal effort. Recent contact with peonage cases, in which federal officials have been unable to act effectively, has forced the belief that, in this field also, there is very little to choose between federal and state action.

In the last analysis, whether the trial be in the federal court or in a state court, the conviction of mob members will depend upon whether or not local people will come forward and give their testimony freely and frankly, whether local officers will do their sworn duty in gathering this testimony, and whether local jurors will set aside their prejudices and personal feelings to the extent of returning a verdict in accordance with the evidence submitted. In other words, whether conviction is sought for violators of a prohibition act, peonage act, or anti-lynching act, the federal court will hardly be more efficient than the state court in areas where the local sentiment has not reached the point of repudiating the crime.

The one good result of the introduction of the Dyer bill has been that it stimulated discussion and wide publicity.

It was opposed on the plea that the states should handle lynching, and that has contributed to the growth of the feeling that state and local officials are placed under a moral obligation to stamp out the evil.

But there is another side of the picture. Successes in some local efforts to curb Judge Lynch have been as encouraging as the failure of the federal government has been disheartening. Lynching is on the decline, largely because of these local efforts. From 255 victims in 1892, the number has steadily decreased to 57 in 1922, 28 in 1923, and 16 in 1924. Many states, including those of the so-called "Wild West," have reduced the evil to a vanishing point. In Georgia, where the problem is often said to be the most difficult, notable progress has been made. The method of conducting the fight under difficult conditions is worthy of detailed attention.

In 1919 and 1920, when crime was rife in the United States, Governor Hugh M. Dorsey was struggling against the current in Georgia. He had many calls for aid from local communities and much experience in dealing with local officials. Upon leaving the governor's chair he summarized some of his experiences in an appeal to the conscience of the law-abiding element in the state, calling upon them to protect Georgia from the acts of organized mob minorities. He cited 135 cases of injustice to the Negro and stated that there had been 57 lynchings, 14 per year, during his administration. The publication of this appeal in pamphlet form was the opening gun in a long campaign against the lawless element.

Since then three years have elapsed, enough time to judge the effects of this course. Before the publication of this pamphlet over 400 cases of lynching had occurred in the state with only one indictment of mob members. In 1922, instead of 14 lynchings, there were 9, in 1923 only 4, and in 1924 only 2. In four cases indictments have been returned and twenty-two people were indicted. Four have been sent to the penitentiary. In two cases where mobs were unsuccessful their members were sued for damages and eight members of unsuccessful mobs were indicted for assault. In every case there has been a storm of indignant protest from the better element of the community.

"That looks like real progress," is the comment of the *Christian Index*, the official organ of Georgia's Baptists. "One thing is true: The people of Georgia are opposed to lynching. We do not believe that this statement has been made frequently enough. There has not been as much encouragement to stand against mob rule as there should have been."

Before Governor Dorsey's exposé the large state papers published very little concerning mobs either in the news or the editorial sections. Since that time, although there has been less actual violence, the volume of comment and condemnation has been large. Clippings from the Atlanta papers alone fill a sizable scrap book. This publicity has been one of the strong weapons against the mob, for mob members shrink from it. Changes in the public mind are slow and their reflection in the acts of officials and courts are still slower, but it is generally felt in Georgia that there is a distinct trend toward the disfavor of Judge Lynch, and the recital of the outcome of the lynching prosecutions of 1922 indicates beyond doubt that this change is gradually molding the acts of local courts and communities.

Besides the press, another powerful agency is arrayed against lynching as never before. This is the sentiment of the churches. The Southern Baptist Convention has condemned mob violence strongly and this condemnation has found its way to congregations through the pulpit. Another powerful religious organization recently arrayed against lynching is the Southern Methodist Woman's Missionary Council. Their statement of their position is especially strong:

Whereas the defeat of the Dyer anti-lynching bill, which provided for the federal control of lynching, has thrown the whole responsibility back upon each state for removing this hideous crime, therefore:

We do now demand of the authorities of the several states that they make good their claim (that they can control lynching), proving their competency to abolish violence and lynching.

That we formulate plans in behalf of adequate state laws and law enforcement.

Besides these general religious bodies, a number of local presbyteries, synods, conventions, and conferences in the South have spoken against the evil and urged their members to use their influence to abate it. The general federation of churches in the United States, the Federal Council, has committed itself to a five-year campaign against the evil. When these great spiritual currents, which are guided by the churches and by the women, turn against lynching, there can be no doubt as to the final outcome of the struggle to eliminate it.

Throughout the South, county committees on race relations and, in some states, county leagues for the enforcement of law have been organized. They have been most effective in strengthening the constituted authorities in their stand against the mob. A study of the activities of these organizations indicates that more vigorous local action may be expected along two lines. One type consists in strengthening the machinery of law enforcement; that is, imposing penalties on negligent sheriffs, creating state police forces, and providing for the rotation of judges and prosecutors so that some of the effects of local prejudice are nullified. The other type consists of the application of a more militant spirit to the enforcement of law in the courts; that is, conscientious jury service, and service as reviser of the jury list, demand for stringent investigation of lynchings, and law-and-order organizations which pledge themselves to lend active aid to the officers of the law.

Much can be expected from such action. This has been proved in some states. In the far West, where lynching first became prevalent, this form of violent and illegal punishment has almost disappeared. It has been supplanted by a strong system of courts and a greater respect for the lawful processes. In the South, where lynching took hold when the court machinery was weakened by the ravages of the Civil War, the evil has thrived behind a smoke screen of color prejudice. Yet in some of the Southern states it has been successfully attacked.

South Carolina, in 1895, adopted a constitutional provision that the governor could remove any sheriff who permitted a lynching in his county. Since that time lynchings in South Carolina have steadily decreased almost to the vanishing point. By a similar provision, adopted in 1901, Alabama has reduced her number from 12 to 5 per year, and the addition of a state police has further decreased the evil. Since the passage of the state police law in Tennessee, almost four years ago, there have been but two lynchings. Kentucky, Florida, and West Virginia also give their governors power to remove their sheriffs, and movements are on foot to secure the same provision in other states.

The most effective anti-lynching provision is the plan of making the sheriff answerable to a superior authority. A determined sheriff can stop almost any mob. He has the whole manhood of the county at his disposal. One sheriff is known to have stopped a mob by deputizing its leaders to protect the prisoner and telling them that they would be held personally responsible for his safety. Another informed the mob that the jail doors were open to them, but that the prisoner was armed with a riot shot gun and would use it if they entered the front door. They did not enter. A powerful water hose is another excellent means of dispersing a crowd, more effective and less fatal than rifle fire. In short, there are a dozen ways open to a resourceful, determined sheriff. For this reason most preventive laws are aimed at strengthening the hands of the sheriff and providing penalties for his negligence. This remedy is much to be desired because it is designed to stop mobs before they accomplish their purpose rather than to punish them after they have committed murder.

Local action also takes the form of more vigorous investigation of lynchings with the view of punishing mob members. Much of the success along this line in recent years has been due to the activity of prominent local leaders who assist prosecuting attorneys in gathering their facts, and who help to create such a sentiment against lynching that grand juries will indict and petit juries will convict mob members.

Another form of local action consists in protecting the prisoner. In one Georgia county eight hundred men recently organized for this purpose. They were divided in squads and one of these squads was actually on duty at the jail continually. The publication of this fact in the local papers made it impossible for a mob to form. In another county the local interracial committee quieted the mob spirit by offering a large reward for the capture and legal conviction of a criminal. Such local activity is now so widespread that the number of frustrated mobs is greater than the number which are successful.

Thus more efficient state and local action has not only almost abolished lynching in some of the Southern states, but in others it has localized the evil. In Georgia, for instance, an examination of the records for the past 22 years reveals that three-fourths of the lynchings have been concentrated in 36 counties and 67 counties have never resorted to this practice. The proportions run about the same throughout the South. These lynching counties are without exception in rural areas where police protection is inadequate and where the courts are weakest.

Another ten years of vigorous propaganda and prosecution will see the mob spirit thoroughly controlled in the United States. This much-to-be-desired goal cannot be reached, however, without the expenditure of a great deal of effort and energy by the average citizen in the communities where the evil is now localized. It will require daring and skill, and there is enough adventure in matching wits with a mob or facing it boldly to appeal to the American spirit. It is a citizen's fight, and the need for waging war against this enemy which attacks our civilization from within is as great as was that for curbing the raids of the red savage against the early pioneer settlements, for mob violence flouts the law and, if unchecked, it weakens all laws. It is dynamite at the foundations of government. If the fight is not won, there can be no safety under legal institutions and democracy itself is in danger.

BIBLIOGRAPHY

Annual Report of the Georgia Committee on Race Relations, 1922.
Atlanta University Publications 8 and 19, 1904 and 1915.
Commission on Interracial Coöperation. "Black Spots on the Map."
CUTLER, J. E. Lynch Law in the United States.
DORSEY, HUGH M. A Statement as to the Negro in Georgia.
MECKLIN, J. M. Democracy and Race Friction, Chapter IX.
Report of the Georgia Commission and the Survey of Mental Hygiene made by National Committee for Mental Hygiene.
STEPHENSON, G. T. Race Distinction in American Law.
The Negro in Chicago. Chapters I and VII.
WASHINGTON, B. T. The Story of the Negro, Vol. II, Chapter IV.
WILCOX, W. F. Studies in the American Race Problems, pp. 443-476.

TOPICS FOR STUDY AND DISCUSSION

1. Spend some time in a court in which Negroes are tried and make observations on the manner of dispensing justice and the attitude of arresting officers and court officials.

2. From your knowledge of the African background of the Negro discuss the suddenness of his change from tribal customs to United States law: (*a*) in regard to property; (*b*) in regard to family morality; (*c*) in regard to drunkenness.

3. From Negro Population in the United States, 1790-1915, study the crimes for which Negroes are convicted and draw conclusions. Supplement this with a study of a local community.

4. Trace the effect of the four outstanding causes of Negro criminality as they are evidenced in the type of crime for which Negroes are convicted.

5. From your knowledge of the actions of a mob, or from actual observation in a community, discuss the effects of a lynching on publicity given the crime, on respect for law in the community, on the innocent Negro population. When two men have been members of a mob and later one is on trial and the other is on the jury, what will happen? How does this affect the court machinery?

6. Study the distribution of lynching and endeavor to explain it: (*a*) on the basis of presence or absence of Negro population; (*b*) on the spirit of law observance; (*c*) on the strength of the police powers.

7. What are the essential differences and similarities between lynchings, strike mobs, and race riots?

8. Study the case records of a charity organization and determine how legal-aid work would lighten the charity burden.

9. Summarize the anti-lynching activities in the United States.

10. Report on the care of the feeble-minded Negroes. (See Census of Negro Population in the United States, 1790-1915, also reports National Committee for Mental Hygiene.) What effect would better care of this problem have on crime?

CHAPTER VIII

THE NEGRO AND GOVERNMENT

The adjustment of the Negro to federal, state, county, and city governments furnishes one of the most difficult tasks of American politics. If democracy is anything more than an empty formula, it means the equalization of opportunity to the fullest extent consistent with the harmonious development of the whole community. It means that every individual, regardless of his color or creed, should have the chance to develop his capacities in any respect in which his individual development does not infringe upon the opportunities of the whole group. It means that the government shall furnish institutions which will contribute to this development of the citizenry and that, in so far as it is consistent with the welfare of these institutions, the citizens shall have a voice in determining institutional policies and administering them.

NEGRO CITIZENS

On the other hand the duties of citizenship in a democracy imply much more than mere residence. They demand support of the community institutions by contributions of money and service and, in extreme necessity, by bearing arms in their defense. Obviously every population is composed of individuals who vary greatly in the ability to perform these duties of citizenship. At the upper end of the scale democracy places the energetic and able leaders who are chosen by the people as experts in legislative, administrative, and judicial capacities. At the lower end are various classes, such as the criminal, the insane, the feeble-minded, and the unnaturalized foreign born, who are almost completely excluded from any of the privileges of citizenship. Between these extremes the masses of average men participate in varying degrees in the administration of the communal affairs. As democracy evolves in the direction of efficiency, more and more restrictions are placed around office holding in order to insure the fitness of the candidate for the place. Various qualifications are set up for voting, the one most universal being the necessity of paying at least a poll tax toward the support of the government. Other prerequisites which have been imposed in various states are literacy, property ownership, and time of residence in the community.

Notwithstanding all idealistic theories that every man is born free and equal, the enlightened democracy does not treat every man equally with regard to the suffrage, eligibility for office, or even with regard to the right to move freely in the community. If it did so, it would lay itself wide open to the attrition of inefficiency, ignorance, vice, and crime. The one principle which must be observed, however, in determining these restrictions is that of testing the capacity of the individual. Whole classes or groups cannot be restricted without the stultification of democratic principles.

If, therefore, all Negroes were feeble-minded, or all were criminal, or all were unable to pay any tax, there would be no problem concerning their relation to American institutions; they would be automatically excluded. If, on the other hand, they were all property holders, all of average intelligence, all incorruptible, the problem would be equally as simple; they could exercise the full duties, therefore share all the privileges of democracy.

But the situation is not simple in any respect. In the very areas where the Negro is in the majority, his group is less intelligent, less familiar with American institutions, farther down in the economic scale, and most likely to constitute the corrupt mass-voting element. In the areas where the Negro is distinctly in the minority, he is more intelligent, has had more chance to observe the workings of the white man's institutions, is higher in the economic scale, and more fitted in every way to perform the duties of citizenship. Consequently the extent to which Negroes are given a voice in determining policies and administering community affairs varies greatly in different localities. In some states the poll tax is the only requirement which they have to meet in order to vote, and as a result we find that full suffrage is granted in all the Northern and several Southern states. In such towns as Boley, Oklahoma, Mound Bayou, Mississippi, and a number of others where the population is wholly Negro, they are in complete control of affairs, and in every state, Northern and Southern, they vote on the same terms as other property holders in bond issues and school elections.

In the light of these differing governmental attitudes of communities toward the Negro, it is interesting to examine the facts available concerning the ability of the Negro to perform the duties of citizenship and the effect of this performance upon the government, for if democracy is to assume a rational attitude toward this large group of citizens it will be arrived at by a calm consideration of the facts rather than zealous advocacy of idealistic formulæ, or stubborn adherence to partisanship or tradition.

NEGRO TAXPAYERS

As property holders a substantial and growing number of colored people contribute their tax money to the support of their federal, state, county, and city governments. The 218,000 farm owners alone pay taxes on over $200,000,000 worth of land. In addition the growing army (472,000 in 1920) of owners of humble homes and the proprietors of small businesses pay considerable amounts into the public treasuries.

It is difficult to determine the exact amount of these tax payments for several reasons, the principal one being that only three states, — Georgia, North Carolina, and Virginia, — separate the property returned by colored tax payers. In Georgia the real and personal property returned by Negroes in 1921 was $59,000,000 out of a total of $1,200,000,000; that is, about a twentieth of the total. The $69,354,000 worth of real and personal property returned in Virginia is 4.4 per cent, or about a twentieth of the total. In North Carolina they return $106,866,000 of the state's $2,213,755,-000, or 4.7 per cent of the total. Estimating from the actual returns in these three states, and the farms and homes owned in other states, it is safe to say that Negroes return about 8 per cent of the taxable property in Mississippi, 7 per cent in South Carolina, 6 per cent in Arkansas, 5 per cent in Alabama and Louisiana, 3 per cent in Florida, 2 per cent in Tennessee, 2 per cent in Texas, and 1 per cent in Kentucky. A safe estimate of the amount of property which they returned for taxes in the whole country is $650,000-000. Inasmuch as property is never assessed at its full value, this is far below the market value of the property owned by colored people.

This proportion varies greatly within the different states. In certain counties and cities where the Negroes are in the majority, the proportion of taxable property which they return is higher. In Burke County, Georgia, for instance, they return about an eighth of the total, while in some of the mountain counties of that state they return none. In the city of Hampton, Virginia, they return 12 per cent of the property, while in Radford they return only about 2 per cent.

PROPERTY OF NEGROES (CENSUS OF 1920)

State	Percentage of Total Farm Property Owned and Rented by Negroes	Value of Farms Owned by Negroes	Value of Farms Rented by Negroes	Number of Homes Owned by Negroes	Number of Homes Rented by Negroes
Alabama . .	21.5	$29,024,680	$86,826,227	35,402	164,609
Arkansas . .	24.2	45,592,538	135,677,516	27,158	83,154
Florida . . .	6.2	9,027,953	7,522,915	22,533	57,203
Georgia . . .	28.0	45,486,236	275,510,473	40,203	225,250
Kentucky . .	2.9	16,391,297	18,996,335	19,372	41,502
Louisiana . .	22.7	25,472,623	81,347,335	28,906	129,088
Mississippi .	51.1	56,751,385	343,737,036	36,449	179,954
North Carolina	21.4	58,659,868	169,844,814	45,909	105,197
South Carolina	35.7	59,839,583	228,363,624	36,519	140,235
Tennessee . .	8.8	25,277,345	64,349,200	28,070	79,907
Texas . . .	6.1	68,170,518	155,175,385	49,550	116,949
Virginia . .	9.8	57,085,473	41,573,389	61,307	84,071

But the property which is on the tax books in the name of colored owners is by no means a complete gauge of the tax borne by colored people. For every dollar's worth of land owned there is approximately three dollars' worth rented by colored farmers; for every home owned there are three rented, and it is a well-established economic fact that on city rental property, although the landlord actually hands over the tax money to the collector, his ability to pay rests on the payment of the rent by the tenant. Likewise the taxes on corporate property and the license taxes are paid by the patrons of the businesses, and the colored people bear their proportionate part. A fair method of arriving at the proportion of the total tax borne by colored people, therefore, would be to add to the value of real property owned, the value of homes rented, and the personal property, and to find what proportion this sum is of the total property.

Such large contributions from colored taxpayers to the support of their governments certainly merit consideration when funds are appropriated for public institutions. Justice and honesty should demand that the Negro get from the government services at least in proportion to the amount of tax which he pays directly and indirectly. The democratic theory of public expenditure demands more than common justice. It demands that the money raised from public taxation be spent where it is most needed, regardless of the sums which the needy group have paid in. If the policy of expending money for education in proportion to the amount paid in were adopted, then the rich districts and wards would have magnificent palaces for public schools and the poorer districts and wards would have schools little better than those provided for the Negroes now. In order to equalize the opportunities in rich and poor counties almost every state has a state school fund which is distributed to these counties not on the basis of what they pay into the state treasury, but on the basis of their school population or school attendance. This would seem to be a fair basis for the counties in turn to use in equalizing the opportunities in their poorer and richer school districts.

Some communities are, however, so far behind the realization of this democratic ideal that it is necessary to hold up before them the amount of money which the Negroes actually contribute in order to emphasize the fact that common justice demands the more liberal support of colored institutions.

Many communities in the South have never expended a cent of public money for a colored public school building, but have relied on the use of a church or a school building erected by private agencies. In some of these communities bonds have been issued recently to build expensive schools for whites. This means that colored property holders are taxed to build school buildings for white people — a condition which is not only undemocratic and unjust, but also unworthy of the essential love of fair play of the American.

When, however, other institutions than the common schools are considered, it is evident that in the majority of Southern states and local communities there are appropriations from which the Negro receives less than justice. For institutions of higher education, that is, the universities, normal schools, junior colleges, agricultural and mechanical schools, and special institutions in Georgia, the Negroes receive only a thirty-fifth of the appropriation, though they pay a twentieth of the taxes directly and bear a much larger part of the tax burden.

The distribution of funds for the benefit of the two races in reform schools, asylums, institutions for feeble-minded, schools for blind and deaf, tuberculosis sanitaria, and other state institutions is more difficult to determine because, in many instances, the Negroes are cared for in special wards of one general state institution, and the one budget includes both races. We may note, however, that only Virginia, Kentucky, Oklahoma, Tennessee, and South Carolina have provision for the institutional correction of Negro delinquent girls. In no state is there an institution for the Negro feeble-minded.

When the local communities are considered there are still other inequalities in the distribution of public funds. Appropriations for parks, almshouses, hospitals, libraries, and other civic improvements should be very carefully scrutinized to see that the Negro has his share of the benefits, at least in proportion to his contribution to the public treasury, if not in proportion to his great need for such institutions.

NEGRO PATRIOTS

In the defense of his country the Negro also measures up to the standard required of a citizen. Those who doubt the loyalty of the Negro to his country or his willingness to lay his life on her altar need only to trace his record in battle. Comparatively few remember that it was Crispus Attucks, a former slave, who was the first to fall in the Revolutionary War; or that Peter Salem, one of a company of Negroes in the battle of Bunker Hill, fired the shot which killed the

British leader, Major Pitcairn, and turned the tide of that
battle; or that the song, "The Old Flag Never Touched
the Ground, Boys," originated from the saying of standard
bearer Carney, who, at Fort Wagner, though severely
wounded and nearly exhausted from loss of blood, held the
flag of his regiment on the parapet until the regiment was
relieved; or that a Negro officer of the 24th infantry was
the first to enter the Spanish Block House in the battle
of El Caney and to haul down the Spanish flag; or
that two Negro soldiers of the 369th infantry (15th New
York National Guard) were the first members of the
American Expeditionary Forces to receive the French croix
de guerre.

It is significant that, in spite of the successive war experiences demonstrating the fitness and devotion of Negro
soldiers, each new war finds leaders debating the advis-
ability of the use of Negro troops. As a rule their doubts
have been frankly expressed, not on the ground of fear of
lack of efficiency in colored troops, but on the ground that
inasmuch as the Negro had not been given a full share of the
privileges of the country — had not always been justly
dealt with — he might not be as devoted and loyal as other
Americans. Another fear frankly expressed has been that
if the Negroes should be called upon to fight for the country
they might demand as recompense more privileges than the
country was willing to grant. In other words, when Americans have faced great crises they have felt as a house
divided; they have feared that resentment on the part of
one great group of the population would make them unwilling to defend the country. These doubts as to the use of
Negro troops appeared early in the Revolutionary War,

when in 1775 General Washington and some of his brigadier generals unanimously rejected the idea of enlisting Negroes. The last day of the same year, however, General Washington reversed this policy and issued orders authorizing the enlistment of free Negroes. Although colored body servants were with Southern troops from the beginning of the Civil War, the federal government, unwilling at first to face the question of the emancipation of slaves, declined to use Negro troops, and this struggle had been in progress two years before Negroes were enlisted. Similar doubts were expressed upon the entry of the United States into the World War, but were very early overruled in favor of the fullest use of colored soldiers.

The Negroes' Revolutionary War record begins with the fall of Crispus Attucks on Boston Common and runs through the exploits of the colored company at Bunker Hill, of the colored regiment in the Battle of Rhode Island, and of the Black Legion from Haiti, which covered the retreat of the Americans and French in the battle of Savannah. It is a chronicle of which Americans, black and white, may be justly proud.

In the War of 1812 the two signal contributions of Negroes were service in the battle of Lake Erie, for which they were praised by Admiral Perry, and at the battle of New Orleans, on whose eve General Andrew Jackson spoke to them in these stirring words:

To the men of color — Soldiers! from the shores of Mobile I collected you to arms; I invited you to share in the perils and to divide the glory of your white countrymen. I expected much from you, for I was not uninformed of those qualities which must render you so formidable to an invading foe. I knew you could endure hunger and thirst and all the hardships of war. I knew that you loved the land of your nativity and that, like ourselves, you had to defend all that is most dear to man. I have found in you, united to these qualities, that noble enthusiasm which impels great deeds.

Throughout the bitter hardships of the closing months of the Civil War, Negro troops were used. General Butler organized the first regiments of Louisiana Negroes late in 1862, and a Kansas regiment was organized early in 1863. In less than six months after the first regiment had been mustered in they had participated in six important actions and had acquitted themselves well.

From the time of the Civil War onward, several Negro units were included in the regular army. The 9th and 10th cavalry and the 24th and 25th infantry regiments have a most honorable place in the annals of the regulars, and were assigned important duties in the Cuban campaign and in the Mexican punitive expedition.

The most remarkable work done by colored troops, however, was during the World War, when 342,000 were mobilized for a great variety of services. At home the active contributions of colored citizens to increased agricultural and industrial production, to Red Cross work, food conservation, and government loan campaigns were a source of pride and a gratifying surprise to those who had not informed themselves on the Negro's patriotism. War records for driving piles and driving rivets fell before the vigor with which Negro workers approached their task. It was a Negro bank of Portsmouth, Virginia, which sold $100,000 worth of Liberty Bonds, though its quota was only $5700, thereby winning first place from all banks in the United States. It has been estimated that the average contribution from Negro men, women, and children to war work funds was $25.

The selective service boards certified 31.7 per cent of Negro and 26.8 per cent of white draftees for full military service. This larger proportion of Negroes indicates a commendable refusal of many colored draftees to claim exemption.

No one who entered or left through one of the great base ports in France can forget the bustling activity and the tuneful singing of the Negro stevedores and labor battalions which, under the direction of American engineers, revolutionized the operation of these ports and opened the eyes of the world to the possibilities of efficiency in unloading ships.

Negro combat troops also were employed. Undoubtedly mistakes of the kind which are unavoidable with green troops were made, but the War Department records show that on the whole these troops, like the white American regiments, acquitted themselves on the field of glory not only with merit, but also with distinction.

The colored combat units were designated as the 93d provisional division (infantry only) and the 92d division (complete). The four infantry regiments (369th, 370th, 371st, and 372d) of the 93d were among the first to embark and were brigaded with the French. The 369th was brigaded with French Moroccan troops and, in the Champagne drive, the whole regiment behaved with such gallantry and courage that 171 of their number were given the croix de guerre and the colonel was awarded the Legion of Honor. This regiment was the first allied unit to reach the Rhine (in front of Laon), and it is said that they "never lost a foot of ground nor a man captured." At one time when the French were hard pressed they held a sector for three months without relief. In the farewell order to the 371st and 372d, General Coybet of the 157th French Division d'infantrie said, "Never will the 157th Division forget the indomitable dash, the heroic rush of the American regiments up the observatory ridge and into the Plains of Monthois. Through their steady devotion, the 'Red Hand' Division for nine whole days of severe struggle, was constantly leading the way for the victorious advance of the Fourth Army."

The 92d Division, composed of the 365th, 366th, 367th, and 368th infantries, with trains and machine gun battalions, was first in the St. Die sector, then at Marbache, before Metz, where they engaged in some heavy action. The casualties of this division were 103 officers and 1543 men. One whole battalion of the 367th was cited for bravery and awarded the croix de guerre, and General Pershing said to them in their farewell review: "You stood second to none in the record you have made since your arrival in France."

No one who reads this record need fear that the Negro is lacking in patriotism or in ability to bear arms for the nation. In all this long military service there has never been a Negro spy or traitor and few have been captured. After each war they have returned to the peaceful pursuits and violence has been put aside. Thus, though denied the fullest participation in the privileges and liberties of America, they have given freely when they were called upon to defend these privileges and liberties.

NEGRO VOTERS

These contributions of the Negro to the support and the defense of the government bring about a paradox in democracy, for there are numbers of communities in which the colored man's ability to support and to defend the government is fully recognized, but in which his privilege of voting to determine policies and to choose officers is flatly denied.

It is significant that this denial is strictest in the areas where the Negro forms a very large proportion of the population. In these communities, the decision as to the Negro's participation in government rests finally upon the actual effects which this participation would have upon the public institutions and public life. The condition is one which calls for supreme wisdom, supreme forbearance, and a supreme determination to preserve the institutions and ideals of democracy against the corruption and inefficiency of mass ignorance on the one hand, and against demagoguery, prejudice, and exploitation on the other.

Back of this situation is the bitter history of reconstruction days when the federal government insisted upon the immediate, idealistic application of the principles of universal suffrage to the illiterate and inexperienced freedmen, and when as a result the South saw exploitation and corruption placed in power, public office debauched, public appropriations lavished, and public faith in government destroyed.

Some escape from such an intolerable situation was imperative. Because the federal constitution forbade discrimination on account of race or color, the reaction in the South was in the direction of the disfranchisement of ignorance and poverty, which, at first, was a virtual disfranchisement of the Negro.

The three classes of restriction which the disfranchisement movement of the 1880's and 1890's placed upon the suffrage were: Requirement that the voter own a stipulated amount of property, demonstrate ability to read and write, or to interpret the constitution of the United States. Since such a large proportion of the Negro population was, at that time, illiterate and since such a large proportion owned no property, they were automatically disfranchised. The door was not, however, closed to them for all times, for, under the law, when they become property owners and when they become trained, they are privileged to apply for registration as qualified voters. It would prove interesting if students of politics could give an accurate picture of the extent to which Negroes have succeeded in registering and in voting under these stringent rules. Where there are two parties, as in Tennessee, Kentucky, Oklahoma, and parts of Virginia and North Carolina, a considerable number of colored registrants vote in all elections. In other states considerable numbers vote on bond issues and local matters but do not take the trouble to vote in general elections because the one-party system is such that the democratic nominee is virtually conceded the election, and very few votes, white or black, are cast except in the primary. In the absence of any recent investigations of this subject the writer may state that it is his personal observation that some 3500 Negroes are registered in Atlanta, 2000 in Savannah, 1000 in Jacksonville, and proportionate numbers in every city or town.

So far there can be no quarrel with the Southern franchise laws as written. If states decide to limit the suffrage to the property holding and intelligent citizens, they are well within their rights and, according to many students of political science, are acting the part of wisdom, for ignorance and irresponsibility are dangerous forces to be loosed in a democracy.

But the administration of these laws was placed in the hands of local registration boards with wide discretionary powers. Where these boards are fair, applying the law to white and colored illiteracy and irresponsibility alike, they serve as a protection of the suffrage. In areas where the Negroes are in the majority, however, or where they form a very large minority, these boards resort to many subterfuges to let in white registrants and rule out colored registrants. In these communities the basis upon which these local boards proceed is that of experience. The bitternesses of reconstruction, the realities of the degradation of politics by the sudden enfranchisement of the masses of black illiterates are too close at hand for them to desire a second experiment in extending the suffrage too rapidly to the masses of colored citizens. Such communities need, however, to weigh carefully the ultimate results of this policy. To quote from Dr. Edgar Gardner Murphy's Present South:

Before all questions which touch the political status of any race or class of men there arises the primary question as to the effect upon our country and its constitution, upon its civic customs and its habits of thought, of the creation of a serf class, a fixed non-voting population.

Another restriction which disfranchises fully as many white people as Negroes is one which is wisely calculated to combat corruption. During the halcyon days of universal suffrage it was common for political henchmen the day before the election to corral large groups of men, march them to the registration booths, give them money to pay their poll tax, and vote them *en bloc*. In order to prevent this, most states require that the poll tax be paid from three to six months in advance of the election. No boss will trust a corrupt voter for such a long period and hence none will advance his poll tax. This requirement restricts the suffrage to the conscientious, far-sighted citizens who form the regular habit of paying the poll tax and registering promptly. With this provision also, there can be no quarrel, as it is usually fairly administered. It is probable that the failure to comply with this provision has more to do with the failure of colored people to vote than any other because the masses of the race do not seem to be nearly so interested in the suffrage as many of their leaders seem to desire.

The third method of excluding the Negro from governmental affairs is the one-party system which has worked out as much to the disadvantage of the white South as that of the Negro. When the literacy and property tests disfranchised the Negro, only the white democrats were left voting and they secured control of the party machinery and determined that the voting in democratic primaries should be restricted to white voters. Legally this is strictly proper, for it is within the rights of a political party to restrict its membership. In practice, however, this has saddled a one-party system on the Southern South which vitiates political life. Where there is just one party, issues are purely local and in most cases they are entirely obscured by personalities. Demagoguery is enthroned and machine government thrives. Thus in closing the front door to ignorance and unreliability, the Southern democratic party has encouraged mediocracy and opened the back door to boss rule and election on petty personalities.

There is much discontent abroad in the South concerning this one-party system. Its evils are keeping good men from seeking office and even preventing them from voting; and there are no counteracting vital public issues to attract them to the political arena. Many people feel that the solution of the situation is the development of two or more parties in the South, and there is no doubt that if the bugaboo of Negro domination were dispelled, the solid South would split, — at least on local issues. It is, therefore, apparent that in excluding the Negro the South is, in a way, politically dominated by the Negro question. Before all others it looms as the bulwark of the one-party system. It was a determining factor in the prohibition vote. It affected the South's stand on woman suffrage and it ramifies into hundreds of questions of public policy, it influences the South's position on child labor, it is a stumbling block in the administration of compulsory school laws, standing as an ever-present shadow across the door of political councils.

The present status of Negro participation in government may, therefore, be stated as one of change, — of transition from the complete disfranchisement of the 1880's and the 1890's to some status of limited franchise under legal eligibility tests.

It may be said, in passing, that politics and the race question do not mix well. In fact, when the mixture is attempted, both politics and the race question suffer. It would seem, therefore, that the evolution of the Negro's place in government must be by the processes of growth rather than by any sudden universal enfranchisement, especially in those communities where the most ignorant and the most backward colored people are massed and constitute a majority. Any agitation on the part of Negro leaders for sudden enfranchisement of the masses only tends to cement the determination of these communities to go to any lengths rather than permit it. On the other hand, the more rigid the regulation against Negroes voting the more they want to vote and the more they magnify the demand for the ballot out of all proportion to its real significance as a means to progress.

For the nation, therefore, the fair position would seem to be that the South is entitled to work out this extremely important and extremely delicate question in the way in which they have begun, without further disastrous interference such as occurred during the reconstruction period. For the white South, what is needed above all is fairness, a determination to enforce suffrage tests equitably on white and black alike, and a resolve to break away from the one-party system and to regain preëminence in the national forums of political action by building a political system around the live national issues and forgetting the more or less dead issue of Negro domination. For the Negro himself the need is for patience, increasing emphasis on the duties of citizenship, and a faith in democracy deep enough to carry conviction that participation in the government will be extended as rapidly as it can be done without the precipitation of reactions which would be harmful to the community as a whole and to the Negroes themselves.

BIBLIOGRAPHY

BRAWLEY, BENJAMIN. A Short History of the Negro, Chapter XIII. Census of Wealth, Debt, and Taxation.

DuBois, W. E. B. Negro Landholder in Georgia.

HAYNES, G. E. The Trend of the Races, Chapter IV.

LONG, F. T. (Phelps Stokes Studies #5, University of Georgia.) The Negroes of Clarke County, Georgia, during the Great War.

MORTON, R. L. History of Negro Suffrage in Virginia Since the Civil War.

Reports of the State Boards of Control, Education, Health and Public Welfare.

Reports of the State Tax Collectors of North Carolina, Virginia, and Georgia.

SCOTT, EMMETT. History of the Negro in the World War.

SNAVELY, T. R. Taxation of Negroes in Virginia.

TOPICS FOR STUDY AND DISCUSSION

1. To what extent is the Negro's present political status complicated by the reconstruction controversies?

2. In what states do Negroes hold what approximates the balance of political power?

3. Study the reports of a state which has separate Negro institutions and determine the extent to which Negroes benefit from state appropriations.

4. From a standard text on economics summarize the theory as to the burden of taxation and discuss the factors which determine the taxes borne by Negroes.

5. Compare the record of the Negro during the World War with that of other groups. What does this indicate as to loyalty?

6. Discuss the proposition that the Negro should receive in appropriations only such amounts as he pays in taxes.

CHAPTER IX

EDUCATION

The racial differences which complicate the tasks of racial adjustment most are the cultural and mental differences. When these are equalized, the Negro is more able to take care of himself. He is a better producer, presents fewer health problems, is less of a burden on the courts, has a fuller religious life, and is less likely to become a dependent or a defective. Education is the greatest force in equalizing these mental and cultural differences. The school aids all other processes of adjustment. When schools are properly developed, churches are stronger, health organizations less burdened, asylums and almshouses emptier, the courts relieved of congestion, and government generally more efficient. Thus education is the greatest of the tasks of racial adjustment.

After years of intimate dealing with public school officials throughout the South, Dr. James H. Dillard, of the Jeanes and Slater Funds, writes:

There has been within ten years, and even more within five years, a decided advance in the readiness and desire of school boards and superintendents to give the colored children a square deal in education. There has been an advance both in length of term in colored schools and in the salaries paid to colored teachers. There has been an advance in the interest taken by superintendents in the better housing and better supervision of the colored schools.

As illustrations in proof of the progressive attitude let me cite three facts. First: Public school officials are appropriating this year $425,000 in coöperation with the Rosenwald donations toward building rural schoolhouses for colored children. Second: Up to seven years ago the Jeanes Fund paid practically all the salary for the rural supervising teachers that were employed in various counties, little or no appropriations coming for this purpose from public funds. This year the public school officials are paying for these workers $120,000. Third: Eight years ago, through the coöperation of the Slater Fund, four graded county training schools were established, to each of which the public school officials appropriated $750, or $3000 in all. This year (1921) the public school officials are appropriating over $650,000 to 141 of such schools.

This quickened interest, especially in the South, in the training of the Negro for more effective citizenship has come partially through the recognition of the essential justice of the plea of the previous chapter for equitable distribution of public funds, and partially through a realization that a better training for Negro citizens will react to the advantage of the whole community. It becomes increasingly clear that ignorance and inefficiency in any class fasten their burdens upon the whole nation and seriously hamper the working of democratic principles.

Many have depreciated and a few still depreciate any effort put forth for Negro schooling. Some of these say that the Negro is incapable of learning beyond a certain point. It was Thomas Jefferson who expressed the belief that no Negro could be found who could trace the propositions of Euclid, and John Calhoun who said that none could give the syntax of a Greek verb. Others fear that education will give him too much power, and still others frankly admit the desire to keep the colored man in the cotton field and state that education spoils a good field hand. Sixty years of Negro schooling have brought results which practically nullify the fears of these doubters. A sufficient number of Negroes have gone through colored colleges and even through some of the larger Eastern universities to dispel any doubt as to the ability of at least a considerable proportion of the race to assimilate a higher education.

NATIVE MENTAL ABILITY

It is known that there are differences in the native mental ability or intelligence of the two races, but just what these differences are, in quantity or in quality, is not known. They are, however, not great enough to warrant any assumption that training along the same fundamental lines as that given to white children will not be beneficial to colored children.

In fact, as Woodworth points out, the world's peoples have essentially similar mental equipments. All have the same senses, instincts, and emotions; all can remember past experiences, and all can imagine objects not present to the senses. All can discriminate, compare, reason, and invent; and in all one impulse can inhibit another. To his mind, the important racial differences are those by which some individuals apply their powers in utilizing certain materials more successfully than others. While one may be gifted in mathematics another will show a special aptitude for music.

According to his experiments, there is much overlapping in racial groups. When a specific mental trait is used as the basis of comparison, one group may show a lower average than another, but the superior members of the lower group surpass the inferior members of the higher group. This is true of brain weight which "would seem to be a trait of great importance in relation to intelligence." The average weight of the Negro brain is about two ounces lighter than the average of white brains, but the variation in each group is about 25 ounces. Thus the heaviest Negro brains considerably outweigh the lightest white brains.

Primitive races are commonly reputed to be far superior to civilized people in their sensory powers, but tests made by the same investigator in this field showed that the popular assumption was erroneous. While the Indians, Filipinos, and other primitive peoples averaged stronger in vision than whites, the members of these groups who were weaker in vision than the average were considerably weaker than the stronger visioned members of the white group. This same overlapping relationship held in experiments with the other senses.

Measuring intelligence is, therefore, a most intricate task, one requiring quantitative tests made on large numbers of individuals by trained scientists. The closest approximation of such a scientific standard was developed in the army mental tests which were given to the recruits drafted for service in the World War. While these tests were primarily designed to measure military value, many commentators take them as a measure of native mental ability, or intelligence. They furnish data based upon a large number of cases, gathered by trained pyschologists. Their results have been painstakingly compiled by Yerkes. They show a considerable difference in the scores made by white and colored soldiers. Of the representative sample studied, only 21 per cent of the Negroes made average or superior scores, while 79 per cent made inferior scores. Of the whites, 76 per cent made average or superior scores, while 24 per cent made inferior scores. Even in this test, it will be noted that there was much overlapping, since the highest 21 per cent of the Negroes ranked above the lowest 24 per cent of the whites.

When quantitative differences in the army tests were equalized by comparison of white and colored men who made the same total scores, it was found that Negroes excelled the whites in certain types of tests, while the whites excelled in other types. This indicated that there are also qualitative differences, and these, in the opinion of many students, will be found to constitute the important distinctions in racial intelligence. When they are thoroughly defined they will be the guideposts to the special capabilities of the Negro and will enable him to find his proper niche in American life.

There are, however, grave doubts as to the fairness of using the army mental tests or, for that matter, of using any mental tests yet devised, as indices of the relative native mental ability of two races. These doubts arise from the fact that it is exceedingly difficult to test native intelligence apart from learning. The army tests show that the educated soldiers measured higher in intelligence than the uneducated. This result leads to the supposition that they tested not native capacity alone, but native capacity plus a coefficient of schooling.

If that is the case, it is to be expected that the Negroes with less home training and less schooling would, apart from any differences in native mental capacity, make a lower grade than the white soldiers. It would also be expected that the Northern Negro, with relatively more schooling, would test higher than the Southern Negro, and an examination of the results of the army tests shows that to be true. The score made by the Northern Negroes averages about halfway between the average of the white soldier and that of the Southern colored soldier. Until psychological tests are further revised so as to measure the factors of native mental capacity more accurately and separate them more sharply from the learned reactions, other comparisons made between white and colored groups, with differing degrees of home and school training, will be subject to the criticism that they do not measure the inborn racial differences, but measure the relative amounts which the individuals have been able to learn.

Making due allowance for the differences in score which may be due to differences in training, the net results of these tests may be summed up as follows: They justify the presumption that some mental differences exist. They lead to the supposition that the important differences are probably qualitative rather than quantitative, and they indicate that these differences are not sufficiently marked to warrant the previous popular assumption of the essential inferiority of the Negro mind, and certainly not sufficiently marked to justify the current belief of the past generation that the majority of Negroes are not capable of profiting by an education.

FEARS OF NEGRO EDUCATION UNFOUNDED

It is true that education does give the individual Negro more power, but this is by no means disadvantageous to the white man. The trained man, white or black, is more valuable to his community; and the trained colored man, if his training has been sound and has included character building as well as learning, is the natural leader of his own people and may be depended upon to lead them in paths which are harmonious with the development of the whole community. The trained leader is more self-controlled. This manifests itself in the clean record of the large number of educated Negroes. Only a negligible number of the thousands of graduates of Hampton, Tuskegee, and the colored colleges have ever become involved in difficulties with the law, and the records of one of the oldest medical schools show that only one of their 2500 graduates has ever been arrested. The Negro's increased power of self-control, and increased power over material things certainly do not work a disadvantage to the white man, while increased power to know his situation and adapt himself to it makes him a much more valuable member of the community.

The fear of spoiling a good laborer by education is extremely short-sighted. The South cannot advance in efficiency until the Negro is better trained. If there is any doubt as to the value which training adds to the work of a colored man, it can be dispelled by an examination of railroad wages. So-called soulless corporations do not pay by sentiment. They arrange their wage scale according to the values which the services of various laborers create for them. With this in mind the traveler can observe the railroad track laborer, an unskilled workman with little training. His wage is proportionately low. Then there is the train porter, more highly trained, more efficient in service, and twice as well paid as the section hand. Then, if the traveler is in the South, the chances are that there is another Negro in the cab of the engine, — the fireman. He must be strictly trained for his job, trained to know the road and to know his engine. He must be proficient enough to enable him, in case of accident, to assume the duties of the engineer and to bring in the precious burden of the train. He, accordingly, is twice as well paid as the porter and four times as well paid as the section hand. The difference in pay of these men is based on their difference in value to the railroad and their difference in value is largely a product of difference in training. In other words, education takes a dollar a day man and makes him worth four dollars a day.

Thus it is apparent that the depreciators of Negro education use very shallow arguments. Their assertions as to the essential inferiority of the Negro mind do not rest upon verified facts, and their fears that education damages the Negro and damages the community can be dispelled by actual observation of trained Negroes at work.

The two great tasks which confront the educators of the colored population are: (1) Provision of a training for the masses which will lift their general standard of living and prepare them to do their everyday job with more efficiency and more character. (2) Provision of a training for the leaders which will enable them to encourage and aid their people on the upward path. This involves special training for teaching, preaching, medicine, and other fields of professional service.

Weakness of Public Schools

The training of the masses is, of necessity, the job of the public schools. Public school systems, even for white pupils in the South, are still relatively backward in their development. It was only in the decade from 1865 to 1875 that elementary schooling was made public on a state-wide basis, and only recently have some states extended aid to high schools. The South is further burdened with the necessity of supporting a double system of schools from woefully inadequate revenues. Before the Civil War it was the richest section of the nation. The war, however, destroyed this wealth and the South became the poorest section. From 1870 to 1900 Southern states were actually poorer in per-capita wealth than they were in 1860. In the meantime other sections of the country had been steadily forging ahead in the accumulation of wealth.

The newness and the comparative poverty of Southern public school systems are great drawbacks to Negro education. In some communities there is also an indifference to Negro education which leads to an unjust distribution of the limited school funds. Notwithstanding these influences the finances of the colored public schools are steadily improving, but are still woefully inadequate for meeting the great needs of the two and a quarter million educable Negro children.

The expenditure for white schools in the South is meager enough in comparison to the expenditure in other sections, but the following table indicates that the expenditure for Negroes is far lower than that for white people. The per capita for the South as a whole in 1922 was $29.72 for each white child and $7.12 for each colored child 6 to 14 years of age. The ratio of white expenditure to Negro expenditure ranges from over 8 to 1 in South Carolina to about 2 to 1 in Oklahoma and Tennessee and almost equal in Kentucky.

EXPENDITURES FOR TEACHERS' SALARIES IN PUBLIC
SCHOOLS PER CHILD SIX TO FOURTEEN YEARS OF AGE

STATE	YEAR	PER CAPITA		PER CENT OF INCREASE	
		White	Negro	White	Negro
Oklahoma . . .	1912–1913	$14.21	9.96		
	1920–1921	41.94	24.85	196	149
Texas	1913–1914	10.08	5.74		
	1922–1923	32.45	14.35	222	148
Kentucky [1] . . .	1911–1912	8.13	8.53		
Tennessee [1] . . .	1913–1914	8.27	4.83		
North Carolina .	1911–1912	5.27	2.02		
	1921–1922	26.74	10.03	407	397
Virginia	1911–1912	9.64	2.74		
	1921–1922	28.65	9.07	197	231
Arkansas . . .	1912–1913	12.95	4.59		
	1921–1922	20.60	7.19	59	56
Louisiana . . .	1911–1912	13.73	1.31		
	1922–1923	36.20	6.47	104	393
Florida	1910–1911	11.50	2.64		
	1921–1922	37.88	6.27	229	138
Georgia	1911–1912	9.58	1.76		
	1921–1922	23.68	5.54	147	215
Mississippi . . .	1912–1913	10.60	2.26		
	1921–1922	28.41	4.42	168	96
Alabama . . .	1911–1912	9.41	1.78		
	1921–1922	22.43	4.31	138	142
South Carolina .	1911–1912	10.00	1.44		
	1921–1922	30.28	3.63	202	152

[1] Per cent figures not available.

These figures are encouraging in that they show that
during the past ten years there have been substantial increases in the per-capita expenditure for Negro children.
This increase has, however, not been sufficient to correct
the discrepancy between the expenditures for white and
colored education because the white expenditures have

also been increasing at a rapid rate. It is interesting to note that in several of the States the expenditure for Negro schools in 1922 just about equaled the expenditure for white schools ten years before.

The variation in expenditure from state to state is subject to further variation in counties. The Black Belt counties do far less in proportion for their great mass of Negroes than do the counties with a lighter percentage of colored population.

PER CAPITA EXPENDITURE FOR TEACHERS' SALARIES IN COUNTIES GROUPED ACCORDING TO PERCENTAGE OF NEGROES IN THE TOTAL POPULATION

United States Bureau of Education, Bulletin 38, 1916

	WHITE PER CAPITA	NEGRO PER CAPITA
Counties under 10 per cent Negro . . .	7.96	7.23
Counties 10 to 25 per cent Negro . . .	9.55	5.55
Counties 25 to 50 per cent Negro . . .	11.11	3.19
Counties 50 to 75 per cent Negro . . .	12.53	1.77
Counties 75 per cent and over	22.22	1.78

It is very significant that counties containing over 50 per cent of Negroes in their population spend so much on white pupils and so little on Negro pupils. This means that in the country districts of these counties a few expensive schools are maintained for the scattered white pupils, while the congested Negroes can be herded into small one-teacher schools with wholly inadequate equipment. State school funds are distributed to these counties on the basis of their combined white and black school population or attendance. In other words, they receive as much from the state fund for each colored child as they do for each white child. The local school board then takes the state fund, adds a local tax, and apportions it to white and colored schools as they please. Justice should demand that such funds be apportioned more closely in proportion to the population of the two races.

Many school districts own no school for colored pupils, but use a church, abandoned cabin, or lodge hall. This property is wholly unsuited to school purposes and is a mere make-shift. The rooms are poorly lighted, equipped with rough, wooden, backless benches, and sometimes utterly lacking in sanitary facilities. Many of the buildings which are owned by the county are in little better condition. A compilation of the amount invested in public school buildings in the fifteen Southern and border states shows a value of $327,067,500 for white schools and $27,828,000 for colored schools, or about $65.50 for each white child of school age and $8.28 for each colored child. This average includes city schools. If rural schools were valued separately and the border states eliminated, the investment per colored child in the rural South would be about $3.50. In other words, the average value of a rural school building serving a typical district of one hundred and fifty children is about $525. There is no need to dwell upon the limitations which such a poor plant imposes in the way of inadequate lighting, seating, ventilation, and sanitation.

Limited funds also make it impossible to operate the schools in the country and in small towns for the full term of nine months. The United States Bureau of Education estimates that the average time during which schools are open in the South is one hundred and twenty days for colored pupils and one hundred and forty-five for white. For the colored pupils this runs as low as four months in

South Carolina and as high as seven months in Virginia and seven and half in Oklahoma.

Furthermore, the attendance is very irregular in the country districts where pupils are often withdrawn to help with the farm work. This is especially true of tenant districts. Pupils, therefore, do not get the full benefit even of the short term offered. The Bureau of Education estimates that the average time that colored pupils are actually in attendance is eighty days per year, or four months. On this basis it would take eighteen years for the average colored pupil to complete the full elementary course of eight nine-month school years. That is to say, he would be about twenty-four years old before entering the high school. This condition, however, is rapidly improving, as it was only a few years ago that the colored attendance averaged only about fifty days per year.

Colored public schools are also handicapped by the poor quality of teaching. While there is an increasing number of devoted, fairly well-trained teachers, the majority of them are concentrated in the towns. There are 35,000 teachers in colored public schools, and only a very limited annual output from teacher training schools to maintain this force. In addition the low pay often makes it impossible for a girl from outside the community to come in and pay board. This means that in many cases the teacher must be found within the community. It happens, therefore, that hundreds of these rural schools are taught by young girls whose training has been limited to that given in the local schools. The average colored rural teacher has less than a full grammar school training and little special preparation for teaching.

Until ten years ago, when county training schools were established, there were no rural high schools for colored pupils, and city high school facilities were very limited. In one Southern state, as late as 1914, there was only one town which provided a full public high school course and there was no rural district with such provision. Rapid progress has been made in this line recently, but much remains to be done. Cities of the type of Louisville, Richmond, Norfolk, Raleigh, Charleston, Atlanta, Jacksonville, Birmingham, Nashville, New Orleans, Memphis, Dallas, Houston, Fort Worth, Oklahoma City, and Little Rock are rapidly correcting this defect in their public school systems. The smaller towns of Virginia, North Carolina, Kentucky, Tennessee, Arkansas, Oklahoma, and Texas, are also making some progress, but there are fully two million colored children living in small towns and country districts where their educational opportunities are limited to a meager elementary schooling.

The reports of the United States Bureau of Education show that in the United States there are 19,428,000 white pupils, of whom 1,829,500 (or 9.4 per cent) are in high school, while only 27,631 (or 1.3 per cent) of the 2,150,000 colored pupils are receiving this training.

Fair dealing demands that public high schools for colored pupils should be developed as rapidly as possible. As a measure for training a valuable group of local Negro leaders the expansion of the high school program is also needed. These schools are the principal agency for training teachers and skilled workers, and as long as many Negroes never can and never will go to college the secondary school will be the training ground for local leaders.

To perform this function effectively, these schools should be much broader in scope than the strictly college preparatory institution. Increased emphasis should be given to history, civics, economics, and the natural sciences, so that everyday life will be more intelligently appreciated. The stimulation of race pride demands that colored pupils be taught more of the history and achievements of their own race. The growing body of literature by colored writers should be studied and the accomplishments of colored men of mark held up as inspiring examples. The exact nature of these special adaptations of the curriculum of colored schools, and the extent to which such adaptations are lacking, are fully developed in the report on Negro education compiled by Dr. Thomas Jesse Jones for the United States Bureau of Education.

Since the masses of rural Negroes are farmers, and since the majority of those in cities are engaged in manual labor, vocational training is of great importance. Manual arts, domestic arts, and agriculture deserve a much more prominent place in the program than they now occupy. There is a widespread general interest in the industrial training of the masses of the Negroes, but because this work is slightly more expensive than the teaching of academic subjects it has been slow to spread.

Many of the minor defects in the colored school could be corrected by sympathetic and careful supervision. Left to their own devices, the small rural schools have many unnecessary faults which could be eliminated by proper supervision. It would seem that Southern states and counties, with an investment of about thirty million dollars, and an annual outlay of over fourteen million dollars in colored schools, would insist that their boards of education and superintendents of schools should interest themselves at least to the extent of making sure that the expenditure of this great sum is efficiently administered. Such, however, is not the case. The superintendents who take a really sympathetic interest and a healthy pride in their colored schools do so entirely on their own initiative. This number is, however, increasing. There are many superintendents who, because of pressure of other duties and a few who because of indifference, visit only one or two colored schools each year. Although the superintendent is elected to supervise all public schools, there is little local criticism of a superintendent who neglects the colored schools.

On the whole, when consideration is given to all these discouraging influences which beset the Negro pupil in the way of short terms, poor teachers, inadequate buildings, and equipment, and the unsettled family conditions which often prohibit regular attendance, the progress which he has made in education has been phenomenal. In 1880 70 per cent of the Negroes over ten years of age were illiterate, but in 1920 this percentage had fallen to 22.9 per cent. Such commendable progress is evidently the product of two things: *first*, the deep desire, almost amounting to a passion, for schooling which is widespread among the masses of Negro parents; and *second*, the willingness of communities to provide facilities whereby Negroes may, after a fashion, receive schooling.

But the task still looms large. Illiteracy amounting to 22.9 per cent (or a total of 1,842,161 illiterates) is a menace, especially since census takers enumerate any one as literate who can so much as write his name. Many of the

77 per cent called literate are, therefore, unable to show much greater learning than is required to scrawl their names. Communities suffer the penalty of these conditions. Whether the illiterates are white or black, they bring the inevitable burdens of inefficiency, slovenliness, disease, and immorality. Thus Negro illiteracy constitutes both an enormous moral responsibility for training these belated people and a serious threat to the communities which neglect this training.

Constructive Agencies

The progress which has been made is due to the statesmanlike coöperation between the educational authorities of the states and counties on the one hand, and the philanthropic boards and foundations on the other. These constructive factors are worthy of close study.

State Supervisors of Colored Schools. The creation of the office of State Supervisor of Colored Schools arose from the feeling of Southern state superintendents that state departments of education could be effective in extending a helping hand to the counties in the task of building colored public schools. Through the generosity of the General Education Board, the salaries of such appointees of the state superintendents were provided. They are extremely valuable in stimulating the interest of county superintendents throughout the South, and, in addition, they act as local agents for the Rosenwald School Building Fund, the Jeanes and Slater funds, and other constructive school funds. Although these supervisors have been at work only about ten years, the public school system of every Southern state has felt the imprint of their personality.

The Anna T. Jeanes Foundation, which was established to aid the rural colored school, has been in operation since 1911, and has rendered a sterling service in raising standards, and in stimulating the coöperation of local school authorities. This fund offers aid to the county in employing a supervising teacher who travels among all the schools in the county, encouraging and aiding the rural teachers and assisting in the elementary instruction in manual arts, household arts, and gardening. Some 270 of these teachers are employed by Southern counties and about three-fourths of their salary is paid from public funds. They are, in effect, rural missionaries, and in the great majority of cases they are well trained and devoted.

Slater Fund. This foundation is especially interested in aiding industrial education in public high schools and in private schools. About ten years ago its directors noted the woeful lack of trained teachers and the fact that low pay necessitated the choosing of many teachers from the local community. They, therefore, felt that each county should have some central school whose academic standards should be slightly higher and whose industrial work should be more thorough than the standards and work of surrounding rural public schools. Two hundred and four of these county training schools have been built. The county authorities, the Rosenwald Fund, and the General Education Board coöperate in establishing these training schools. A recent study by Leo M. Favrot shows that while they are still weak in many respects, they represent the nearest approaches to county high and normal schools that are open to the Southern rural Negroes. The public expenditure for developing these institutions is gradually being extended, $594,000 being expended from public funds in 1924 as against $131,000 in 1919. Over 6100 pupils are enrolled in high school grades, and reports indicate that the great majority of county superintendents thoroughly appreciate their value as places to which the more advanced pupils of the county can go and receive slightly better training than that offered by the average rural schools.

Rosenwald Building Fund. In order to stimulate the erection of better rural school buildings, Julius Rosenwald has offered to defray part of the cost (from a third to a fourth of the total) of rural school buildings. As it works out in the community, the Rosenwald Fund usually appropriates about one-fifth, the public funds about one-half, and the white and colored people raise about a third of the cost of these buildings.

Under this plan (up to 1925) 2565 schools have been built at a cost of over $10,000,000, and they are stimulating a wide interest in better construction, better equipment, and better sanitation in colored rural schools. They serve as object lessons for the rest of the county in modern school construction. Over 1000 have a capacity for three or more teachers. No single force has been more influential in improving Negro public schools than the provision of this generous aid in building modern school buildings and the resultant tendency to equip these buildings well and to man them with better teachers.

General Education Board. This board appropriates to the Jeanes Foundation to aid supervising teachers, pays state supervisors of schools, who act as local agents and supervisors for the above funds, and aids with the equipment of county training schools.

Phelps Stokes Fund is a research foundation of broad scope which is interested principally in the larger schools, but which has coöperated in various ways with all the above named foundations. This fund has been valuable in stimulating study of the Negro by white college men.

With all these efficiently directed agencies coöperating closely to promote better state and county supervision, better school buildings, and central training schools in each county, those who are genuinely interested in Negro education can secure valuable aid in launching some community project if they can secure enough local interest to make the community do its part.

State Higher Schools

Negro education must work at the bottom and at the top of the scale at the same time. The primary need is, of course, the training of the masses in the public school, but this is not possible without the simultaneous development of a trained Negro leadership, and especially a trained group of Negro teachers and preachers. The pioneer efforts to develop a public school system are well under way in every state, but, to train leaders, the development of higher and professional schools must go hand in hand with the development of the public school system.

States recognize this policy in their general system of education for white people. State institutions for white people include universities, colleges of agriculture, law, mechanic arts, medicine, dentistry, pharmacy, and normal schools. The demand for Negroes who have the training given in such schools is growing. In the Southern states sentiment will not permit them to attend the same institutions as white people. The South must choose, therefore, between providing a separate system of higher education for Negroes and shirking the moral responsibility for developing a Negro leadership. If this moral responsibility is shirked, then the South is faced with the further practical difficulty of dealing with a colored population whose masses are trained at home in the public schools, but whose leaders, including the teachers of the public high schools, are trained in other states.

This responsibility rests partially upon the whole nation, because the events of the Civil War and reconstruction made the tasks of racial adjustment national in scope, and because recent migrations have made the Negro population national in distribution. The philanthropists of the nation as a whole have shouldered this responsibility for training Negro leaders more whole-heartedly than have the Southern states. The study published by the United States Bureau of Education in 1916 indicated that about half the high school pupils and all but twelve of the sixteen hundred and forty-three college pupils were in private and denominational schools, while the nine hundred and forty-four professional students were all in private schools. In other words, the states have, to date, assumed no further responsibility than that of offering agriculture, trade, and teacher training in conjunction with public high school work.

In each Southern state there is a colored agricultural and mechanical school of secondary grade offering trades, domestic arts, and teacher-training courses. These schools are partially supported by state appropriations and partially by the Morrel Federal Fund for Agricultural and Mechanical Education. In addition, several states maintain separate normal schools for colored people. In proportion to the expenditure for white institutions the support of these colored state schools is very meager.

According to the Bureau of Education report, "The Southern states appropriate annually $6,429,991 for higher schools for white pupils and only a little over a third of a million for higher schools for colored pupils (1914-15)." The amounts have increased since this survey, but the proportion between white and colored remains about the same. In other words, while the Negroes form about a third of the population of this section, they receive only about a sixteenth of the money expended for training above the high school. In one Southern state they form nearly half the total population and own about a twentieth of the property, but receive only one thirty-fifth of the money expended for higher education. In other words, they receive a smaller proportion of the appropriation than that to which their share of the taxes entitles them.

The federal government, through the Smith-Hughes Act of 1917, appropriates money for aid in teaching agriculture, domestic arts, industry, and teacher training. For every dollar of federal money spent, the state or community must spend a dollar. These funds are allotted to the states as follows: for teacher training, on the basis of total population; for agriculture, on the basis of rural population; for trades and home economics, on the basis of urban population. The Negroes are, therefore, entitled to share in these funds on the basis of their proportion in the population.

The need for industrial and agricultural education and teacher training is universally recognized in the South. But Southern politicians have not reached the point of granting the justice of the demand for increased appropriations to meet this need. This condition is, however, changing. Within the past few years several of the state Negro schools have received substantial increases in their appropriations, and there is hardly a state which has not increased its appropriation slightly. In order that practical agriculture may be well taught, that instruction in the trades and household arts be thorough, and that teacher training be modern, there is a great need for an increase both of federal and of state appropriations for the work.

HAMPTON AND TUSKEGEE

In advancing this type of education the ideals of Hampton Institute and Tuskegee Normal and Industrial School have been very influential. Beginning with the pioneer ideas and spirit of General Armstrong's work for freedmen at Hampton and developing and spreading through the growth of that school and through the founding of Tuskegee by Booker T. Washington, these institutions have given the world valuable ideals of industrial training and character building. The work of each is twofold in its significance, as it consists not only of training students within the school, but also of rendering a broader service to the leadership of the colored people by maintaining many extension activities.

These institutions are cities within themselves, each having about eighteen hundred pupils and several hundred instructors. Each has been able to make such a large number of friends for its plan of education that property worth several million dollars apiece has been accumulated, and annual maintenance funds of over three hundred thousand dollars apiece are contributed. The visitor on the campus of either of these schools is inspired by the sight of hundreds of neatly arranged, substantial buildings, many of which have been entirely constructed by the manual labor of the students. Orderly activity is apparent on the farm, in the dozens of trade shops, and in the classroom. Here one feels that the young colored boys and girls are given the opportunity to share in the best which the two races have been able to evolve in education.

Until recently both these institutions have confined their academic work to the high school courses. Within the past few years, however, Hampton has added a college course in order that the academic training of those who go out to teach may be more thorough.

The plan of going to school three days and working at a trade three days in the week has been one of the distinctive contributions of these schools to industrial education. While this has limited the academic training received from book study, it has made for a thoroughness in trade instruction and a type of character building which has produced leaders whose services have been of untold value to the South.

The plan of allowing first-year students who are without funds to work all day and go to school at night opens the door of these schools to energetic youths, even though they be practically penniless; and hundreds, like Booker Washington, lacking even railroad fare, have walked long distances to enter. As a result, they have risen from the bottom to positions of great usefulness.

But the activities outside the walls are as significant as those within. A score or more of small editions of Hampton and Tuskegee have been started by graduates of these schools, and the parent schools are constantly aiding and encouraging these branches. The many teachers, supervisors, farm and home demonstration agents, nurses, tradesmen, farmers, and preachers who have graduated are aided in their services to colored communities by movable schools, farm demonstration service, and frequent conferences and short courses. Arising from Booker Washington's interest in health, the observance of National Negro Health Week has spread throughout the colored population and become an institution. From the business interest has sprung the National Negro Business League. No short chapter could begin to describe and evaluate the manifold activities of these schools. But it may be said that he who would learn of Negro education and Negro progress might well begin his study by a trip to Hampton or Tuskegee.

Private and Denominational Schools

White philanthropists and denominational boards have been very generous in providing for the higher education of colored people. In fact, had it not been for their contributions the facilities for training Negro leadership would be very much undeveloped. The annual income of these private schools is about three and a half million, of which about two and a quarter million is expended in denominational schools and a million and a quarter in independent schools. These institutions care for the entire college and professional training of the Negro. The larger proportion of this money is contributed by individuals and denominations in the North. In fact, of the two and a quarter million expended annually for maintenance of denominational schools, only about $100,000 comes from Southern white denominations, and $500,000 from colored denominations, leaving about $1,600,000 from Northern white mission boards.

For some time after the Civil War these boards gave considerably more than money. They sent some of the choicest spirits in their ranks as missionary teachers. Facing discouragement, ostracism, and many other difficulties, these white teachers preserved the link of connection between the white race and the training of Negroes in the higher schools. They have left their indelible imprints upon such institutions as Fisk, Howard, Atlanta, Tougaloo, Talladega, Lincoln, Straight, Hampton, Clark, and Meharry Medical College, as well as upon a number of smaller denominational high schools. The character and devotion of many of the well-trained Negroes of to-day is due largely to the efforts of these missionaries, and the South and the Negro race owe them much gratitude. As colored people receive more training, these white teachers are gradually being replaced by Negro teachers. But several hundred of them still remain and serve in a spirit of devotion.

As these white teachers are withdrawn there still remains a number of white people who serve on boards of trustees of colored institutions. These are also very useful in maintaining the necessary friendly contacts between the colored schools and the white race.

Most of these higher schools for colored people have been seriously hampered by inadequate funds. This has limited their teaching force, library facilities, and scientific apparatus; and it has, therefore, seriously narrowed the scope of college and professional work. In fact the Bureau of Education's survey disclosed only three institutions whose teaching force and equipment made them worthy of

classification as "college." Since this survey others have
improved sufficiently to receive this classification. Fifteen
others had a comparatively small college enrollment with
large elementary and high school departments, while 15
others offered a few college subjects above their high school.
Thus only 33 institutions at the outside offered any degree
of college training and they enrolled only about 2500 in
college classes, a number entirely inadequate to provide a
corps of trained leaders for ten million people. The need
is not so much for new colored colleges as for an expansion and strengthening of the facilities of the colleges now
established.

The same weakness in social and natural sciences which
was commented upon in the high school is evident in the
colored college. Limited teaching force confines many of
them to the narrow classical college curriculum with much
time devoted to mathematics and foreign languages and
relatively few electives offered. Recent expansions in the
appropriations for these schools have begun to enable them
to broaden the courses which they offer, but most of them
are in need of much greater expansion.

In 1916, excluding teacher training, there were only
1400 students in professional schools of college grade, of
whom 431 were medical, 287 dental, 160 pharmaceutical,
441 theological, and 80 legal. This meager output empha-
sizes the great need for the development of several real
university centers for Negroes, where professional training
could be given along with courses of college grade. No
such center is now available. Atlanta with five colleges,
Nashville with Fisk, Roger Williams, and Meharry College,
and Washington with Howard University offer possibilities

as university centers. The diversity of ownership and control in Atlanta and Nashville have militated against requisite coöperation between the institutions, and the limited appropriations of Congress to Howard University have hampered its development.

When the conditions of Negro education for both the masses and the leaders are compared with their condition forty years ago, it is realized that remarkable progress has been made in the elimination of illiteracy, in the beginnings of a public school system, in establishing policies in trade and agricultural training, and in founding institutions for training leaders. On the other hand, when the facilities for Negroes are compared to the facilities for white people, the stupendous task of Negro education is apparent. The effectiveness of the various funds and denominational boards now at work and the rapidly growing public opinion in favor of greater educational opportunity lead the student to feel that the future will see this task taken firmly in hand.

The $500,000 which the Negroes give annually to schools operated by their own denominations, the $2,300,000 which they have given toward the erection of Rosenwald public school buildings, and the sums which they raise in many communities to supplement the meager public funds and extend the school term a few weeks show that even from their limited means they are willing to contribute for education. The crowding in such schools as they have indicates a burning desire among the parents that their children be educated. A race that shows such a desire to learn and a willingness to take advantage of, and to supplement every opportunity for schooling certainly deserves a chance to lift itself through education.

BIBLIOGRAPHY

BOAS, FRANZ. The Mind of Primitive Man, pp. 17–29 and Chapter V.

Bulletins Nos. 38 and 39, 1916. United States Bureau of Education. "Negro Education in the United States," Vol. I, Chapters I and III. Also consult Vol. II for particular state chapters.

Current Biennial Surveys, United States Bureau of Education. (Facts in this chapter from Bulletin 29, 1923; see pp. 45, 98, 99, 103, 497.)

HAYNES, GEORGE E. The Trend of the Races, pp. 63–79.

MURPHY, E. G. The Present South, Chapter II.

ODUM, HOWARD W. Social and Mental Traits of the Negro.

Reports, General Education Board, Slater, Jeanes, Rosenwald, and Phelps Stokes funds.

State Department of Education Reports.

WEATHERFORD, W. D. Present Forces in Negro Progress, Chapter V.

WOODWORTH, R. S. Racial Differences in Mental Traits. Reprint from *Science*, February 4, 1910.

YERKES, ROBERT M. Mental Tests. Memoirs National Academy of Science, Vol. XV, Part III, Chapters 8 and 10.

TOPICS FOR STUDY AND DISCUSSION

1. From the results of the army tests (Memoirs of the National Academy of Science, Vol. XV, Part III, Chapter 10) study the types of mental tests in which the Negro excelled and the types in which they were excelled.

2. Study the reduction of Negro illiteracy by states. What effect does this have on crime and efficiency? Supplement this with observations in your community.

3. Discuss the difficulties confronting the Negro child who desires an education.

4. Practically all the industrial schools are equipped to teach the hand trades. In the light of the table, Chapter VI, page 110, showing Negro occupations in 1910 and 1920, how well is this teaching adapted to the present industrial situation.

5. In the light of the occupations of Negroes and democratic fair dealing, discuss the merits of the controversy between advocates of industrial and of college education for Negroes.

6. Summarize the activities of the funds interested in Negro education and rate the value of their activities. Trace the effect of each on the colored schools of a particular community.

7. Communicate with Hampton Institute, Tuskegee Institute, or Fisk University, securing data as to occupations of their graduates, and draw conclusions.

8. Discuss the appropriations of your denomination and those of your state to Negro schools.

9. Study the schools of your community and report on: (*a*) condition of building as compared to white buildings; (*b*) length of term; (*c*) training of teachers; (*d*) regularity of attendance; (*e*) high school work; (*f*) industrial work.

CHAPTER X

THE HUMANITARIAN INTERESTS

No phase of race relations touches the heart of the South so intimately as the humanitarian task of alleviating the lot of the unfortunate classes. Although the heart is touched the intellect does not always direct the wisest action. The Negro street beggar is generously provided for, and the "hat in hand diplomat" who applies to "his white folks" usually goes away with everything he has asked for, often with more than he deserves. The liberality with which these colored beggars are treated is often more of a liability than an asset to racial adjustment, because such emotional but unscientific giving often leaves the givers with a paternalistic feeling toward the whole race and a belief that by giving small alms they have discharged their full civic duty toward their colored neighbors.

This kindly, paternalistic spirit in some people and apathy in others has, in a large measure, thwarted the growth of really scientific social welfare work for the unfortunate classes of colored people. But, with the development of organized social work for white unfortunates, some of the old personal kindness is working itself out into service on boards and in organizations for the thoroughgoing care of the poverty stricken, the orphan, the delinquent, the insane, and the feeble-minded colored people.

The younger generation of Negroes is taking much more interest in this type of work among their own people. Formerly this interest was centered, in an unorganized way, in their churches, but it has recently become more specialized, although the colored church is still active in these matters.

RELIEF

The relief of families in distress has been carried on to a greater extent in colored churches than in white churches. Many times a destitute colored family, or one who has knowledge of such a family, appeals to the minister and is allowed to make an appeal to the congregation, after which a special collection is taken. Thus the Negroes have, to a remarkable extent, taken care of their own unfortunates.

This, manifestly, is a haphazard procedure. Money is not always the primary need of a family in distress. Sometimes legal aid would help them more. Sometimes a wandering father or brother needs to be compelled to contribute to their support. In short, in modern organizations, family relief has become a specialized branch of social work with a definite technique. While the generous impulse to distribute alms may give a family temporary relief, it may also tend to sap their self-reliance and make them perpetual beggars. These generous impulses and humanitarian interests are valuable and need to be retained, but they should be guided by a special worker trained to investigate such cases, diagnose their real need, and put them in contact with the agency which can meet that need. As the Southern charity organizations expand they do more and more of this scientific family case work among Negroes.

White workers, however, often find it difficult to secure
the full confidence of colored families or to get an intimate
knowledge of their true situation. The most efficient
family case work among colored people, therefore, requires
a well-trained colored case worker employed by the established relief agencies. Many charity associations are employing such colored workers, but training facilities have been
so limited that most of them have been trained on the job.

Public relief appropriations are also voted in small
towns and counties and colored people occasionally share
in them. This is also a very haphazard procedure and
politics rather than scientific rehabilitation often deter-
mines the distribution of these small doles. The indigent
aged are, for the most part, cared for in county almshouses,
there being only one or two very small institutions built
especially for the aged colored people. The census figures
show that in the South there is a slightly higher proportion
of the colored population listed as paupers in almshouses
than of the white, but a much lower proportion of colored
people than of the foreign-born population.

There is a great need for more information upon this
subject of public poor relief both outside and inside of almshouses in the South. In the absence of any collection of
scientific data in this field very little can be said as to the
status of the relief of the Negro cases. It does constitute
a problem for both the student of politics and the student
of sociology. The masses of colored people are so low in the
economic scale that sickness, sudden loss, and old age often
find them unprepared.

All of their lodges are, however, mutual-benefit societies,
and the small sick and death benefits which they pay often

carry the recipient through a period of misfortune. A tremendously larger proportion of colored people than of white people carry these small mutual-benefit policies. Here again, colored people, without any outside aid, have worked out a mechanism for taking care of their own misfortune, — a means which is peculiarly adapted to the sociability of their temperament and the small wages which they earn. There are hundreds of these orders scattered through the country and the Negro Year Book estimates that they have accumulated about twenty million dollars' worth of property. A number of them are national in scope and enroll several hundred thousand members. It is not at all unusual to find Negroes who work for a very small wage but pay dues in five or six of these orders. In addition to the secret benefit societies, large Negro industrial insurance companies have grown up, and several white companies do a lucrative business writing Negro industrial insurance. The Metropolitan Life alone numbers 1,500,000 Negro policy holders.

ORPHANS

The family ties are very loose among certain classes of colored people and the result is a relatively high illegitimacy rate and a large number of desertions. There is, however, a real sense of responsibility for caring for the children in these cases. Most of this burden falls upon the colored women. When children without father, mother, or near relatives are found, somewhat the same procedure is followed as in relief cases. The minister takes the matter up and finds some motherly soul in the congregation who will care for the child. Too often, however, this woman is one who already has a numerous brood and feels that one more will not bring much added responsibility. There is seldom a careful investigation as to the fitness of the home for receiving the child.

Thus in child placing, also, the colored population, after its fashion, takes care of its own. Very few orphanages have been built, and these few are small. The proverty of the race has saved them from the mistake which the white people have made in building large institutions and herding great numbers of orphans together in them to such an extent that they lack the individual care and the love which come to the child in the home.

There is need for a thorough study and organization of the colored child-placing activities so that the commendable tendency to keep children in normal families may be encouraged and systematized. There is also a field for the limited development of colored orphanages as temporary homes for many children while they are being placed. A few will always be permanently domiciled in the institutions. The visitor to such institutions as the Leonard Street Orphanage in Atlanta, which is a model home in many respects, is impressed with this need for the further development of orphan homes to supplement the development of child placement.

Every Southern state has a child-placing society but none of these employ colored workers or handle colored cases. Thus the colored people are left to their own devices, and while they take care of their own orphans to a remarkable extent, it is not at all uncommon for social workers to discover little black waifs who wander homeless in the cities. There is really no information as to how many such waifs there are or how they manage to exist.

Juvenile Delinquency

The lack of proper reformatory facilities has been mentioned in Chapter VIII. All states have juvenile court laws, but only the larger counties have juvenile courts in the real sense of the word. In the smaller counties, the registrar, the county ordinary, or some other county official is appointed as juvenile judge and he gives only a very small amount of time to the work, usually without the aid of a probation officer. Young Negro offenders are seldom arrested until they become actually obnoxious to the community, and then they are often thrown into jail with hardened criminals to receive their first lessons in crime.

Like the family case worker, the white probation officer often finds difficulty in securing the proper coöperation from colored delinquents, their families, and their neighbors. This creates a real necessity for colored probation officers in large counties, and for voluntary colored advisory committees in the counties where there are only a few colored cases to be handled. The coöperation of these people with the juvenile court brings an intimate understanding and a sympathetic touch to the colored cases which can be gained from no other source.

In the final analysis, the sociologist is primarily interested in preventing the conditions from which disease, poverty, insanity, desertion, and crime arise, rather than merely being contented with attempts to cure abnormal cases after they have developed. This, in effect, means that the tasks of reducing the numbers of unfortunates are primarily those of the agencies for education, public health, improvement of economic life, and living conditions.

One especial line of work which would be of value in aiding to prevent these abnormalities in society would be a campaign by the colored church, school, lodge, and lay leaders to place greater emphasis on the social importance and sanctity of normal family life. Neither African tribal customs nor the customs of slavery tended to inculcate into the Negro the highest ideals of family life. His church and his customs since emancipation have aided greatly in this respect, but further emphasis on the importance of the stability of the home would contribute materially to the reduction of the incidence of disease, poverty arising from desertion, crime, juvenile delinquency, and dependency.

INSANITY AND FEEBLE-MINDEDNESS

Insanity is probably better cared for than any other abnormality of the Negro. The colored wards of all state insane asylums are crowded but usually as well administered as the white wards. Census figures tell very little as to the insanity rate among colored people, but they seem to indicate a somewhat lower rate than that of the white population. This may be due in part to lesser tendency to nervous disorders, and in part to the fact that a larger proportion of the Negro insane are not in institutions but at large in the community. The discrepancy between the rate for Negroes (131.4 per 100,000) and that for foreign-born whites (400 per 100,000) is so large that it is certain that there is a much stronger tendency toward insanity among the foreign-born than among the Negro population.

The index to the number of colored feeble-minded is still less accurate since the census lists a very small number in institutions and these are all in the North. Quite a number of colored feeble-minded patients are in insane asylums, but no Southern state provides a special institution for these defectives and the overwhelming majority are free in the community to breed vice, crime, and more feeble-mindedness.

The interrelation of crime with poverty and feeble-mindedness is well understood and the power of crime, when improperly corrected, to breed more crime, is also a known fact. States, therefore, which do not provide the proper facilities for the reformation of young offenders and for the separation of the insane and feeble-minded from the normal community can hardly expect anything else than high Negro crime and disease rates, for which the final fault rests more upon the negligence of the state than upon any inherent criminality of the Negro race.

As stated in the population chapter, the rapid urbanization of the Negro intensifies these problems of the abnormal classes. The Negro crime rate in the North and West is three times that in the South because the population in the North and West is largely urban. The urban insanity rate is also three times the rural rate. Each disaster to the cotton-growing industry drives thousands of Negro families from settled, quiet country districts, where they have been furnished with a house and with fuel by the landlord, to the hurried city life, where numbers of them make a precarious living by doing odd jobs. They are eternally in difficulties trying to secure funds for paying rent or buying food and fuel. They are herded in insanitary tenements where the opportunities for vice and crime are redoubled. In these social menaces of the city lies the real danger to the colored population of rapid industrialization.

TRAINING FOR SOCIAL WORK

Every Negro leader should have a deeper knowledge and appreciation of social problems. This is especially true of the preachers and teachers because of the direct contact which they have with cases needing intelligent care. Colored colleges and theological schools, however, put little emphasis on the social sciences. The need for colored case workers, probation officers, institutional workers, and other specialists creates a further demand for specialized training in public welfare work.

Little has been done to supply this demand. A few colored students have been graduated from such schools as the New York School of Social Work and the Chicago School of Social Administration, but there is need for a still greater specialization on colored problems than these institutions offer. Good beginnings toward this specialization have been made in Nashville in connection with Fisk University, and in Atlanta, in connection with the colleges and social welfare institutions of that city. The requisites of this training are that both academic work in social sciences and practical observational work in connection with well-established welfare organizations should be offered. Both of these Southern schools for training colored social workers need to be greatly strengthened in order that workers with the proper standards may be supplied to the growing number of welfare organizations which are showing a willingness to specialize on colored problems. Colored colleges also need to impress the importance of this work on their students so that more of them will take it up as a life profession.

The development of high standards in colored welfare institutions will, of necessity, depend largely upon the extension of the recent movement to develop strong state departments of public welfare in the Southern states. North Carolina and Georgia have made substantial progress in this line and there are beginnings in the other states which give great promise of development. The aid and supervision which strong, well-financed state departments can give to local communities in handling their problems of dependency and delinquency is invaluable. Each state department, in states which have a heavy Negro population, should have a specialist in Negro welfare work to study the special problems of that group and stimulate their special activities.

COMMUNITY CHESTS

Probably the most concrete recent movement for stimulating the colored people to greater interest in their own unfortunate classes and for providing an opportunity for white and colored people to coöperate unselfishly in humanitarian endeavor has been the community-chest movement, which is spreading rapidly in the South. These community funds usually include at least two agencies which have a program of welfare work for colored people, — the Associated Charities, and the Tuberculosis Association. Often there is also a colored branch of the Y.M.C.A. or Y.W.C.A. and sometimes a special colored institution, such as the Urban League, or orphanage, or an old people's home.

Without the community chest, the financial support of these colored programs has been extremely precarious and their work has been accordingly hampered. But in the community chest their financial support is assured and they are able to do far better work.

In subscribing funds to these chest campaigns, the Negroes have shown a real eagerness to respond when special effort has been made to secure subscriptions from them. Their contributions as reported by various chests range from 40 to 95 per cent of the budgets of their institutions. They usually pay their pledges promptly. The experience of the Atlanta Community Chest, to which the colored people subscribed 95 per cent of their budget, is worthy of note. This campaign included the Associated Charities, two colored workers; Tuberculosis Association, one colored worker; Travelers Aid, one colored worker; Phyllis Wheatly Branch, Y.W.C.A.; Urban League; Neighborhood Union; and two colored orphanages. Their combined budgets were about $40,000 and the colored people subscribed over $39,000. One colored man alone subscribed $1200, while the employees of one large colored corporation subscribed more than $8000. At no previous time had the colored subscriptions to these institutions amounted to over $15,000 annually.

In this campaign a special colored committee was organized to explain the work of these welfare organizations to their group and solicit subscriptions from them, and the ministers extended their fullest coöperation. The results were not only greatly encouraging to the colored people, who felt that they were carrying their share of the burden and were accorded a fair representation in the councils, but their daily reports to the white campaigners also furnished a fine stimulus to the general campaign, as they demonstrated that the colored population was stretching its thin pocketbook to meet the humanitarian needs of the city.

The organization of the chest was also of great value to race relations because, for the first time, it spread the knowledge of social welfare work widely among the masses of colored people and united them behind their welfare institutions more solidly than ever before. It also brought to the attention of the white leaders the needs of the colored community to such an extent that the colored work is now a definite part of the welfare program of the city. The by-product of such coöperation is a spirit of good will, mutual understanding, and mutual respect which could hardly be secured except through such mutual, unselfish service to the community.

BIBLIOGRAPHY

Census of Benevolent Institutions.
Census of the Negro Population in the United States, 1790–1915, Chapter XVII.
McCord, C. H. The American Negro as a Dependent, Defective, and Delinquent.
Reports of State Departments of Welfare and Health.

TOPICS FOR STUDY AND DISCUSSION

1. What would be the effect on problems of poverty, dependency, insanity, and delinquency of more thorough-going effort to perform the tasks of education, public health, recreation, and economic justice?

2. What institutions or organizations in your community handle cases of Negro relief? Are their efforts directed at rehabilitation of families or merely at giving temporary relief in the form of charity doles?

3. Study the records of a family agency and determine the factors which contribute to Negro dependency.

4. By inquiring among Negro preachers and sick and death benefit societies determine the extent and manner in which the Negro population of a community takes care of its own unfortunates.

5. What is the relation of the problems of the day nursery, the orphanage, and the family relief society?

6. In what respect would a home-visiting teacher attached to the school be able to reach the problems of abnormal families?

7. What is the relation of the neglect of poverty and dependency to crime and delinquency?

8. Study the treatment of juvenile delinquents in your community. Talk with the judge and determine the volume of Negro cases. Has he a colored probation officer, paid or voluntary? What training has the officer had? Has he a colored advisory committee? What is their success in handling cases? What institutions are available for temporary detention of boys, of girls; for reformation of boys, of girls? Is the program designed to prevent delinquency before it occurs or is it designed merely to correct delinquencies already committed?

CHAPTER XI

RELIGIOUS DEVELOPMENT

The church is the most powerful institution in Negro life.

The Negro church is the only social institution of the Negroes which started in the African forest and survived slavery; under the leadership of priest or medicine man, afterward of the Christian pastor, the church preserved in itself the remnants of African tribal life and became after emancipation the center of Negro social life. So that to-day the Negro population of the United States is virtually divided into church congregations which are the real units of race life. — Report of the Third Atlanta University Conference.

A larger proportion of Negroes is reached by the church than by any institution. In fact, the proportion of membership among the Negroes is higher than the proportion in the white population. The Census of Religious Bodies of 1916 showed that 4,602,805 Negroes, about 45 per cent of the total population, were church members. The white church membership was 37,324,049, or about 38 per cent of the total population.

A second source of the power of the church is the strong grip of the religious motive on the emotional nature of the Negro. Because the emotions of the race are so bound up with the religious urge, the church has a great influence on all of its members. They attend regularly and will sacrifice to a remarkable extent to contribute to church activities. The historical background of the race has also made a commanding position for religious expression in the life of the individual. The African medicine man had a monopoly on sorcery, witchcraft, worship, medicine, and advice. Tradition has preserved much of this absorbing importance for the church and the preacher.

The church is also influential in the life of the race on account of its power as a social institution. The Negro has so few institutions, so few gathering places, that the church has become the logical center for community life. In fact observers have frequently noted that the successful Negro church is as much a community center as a place of worship, and the average successful minister is one who stimulates a continual round of activities, devoting as much time to community work as to preaching the gospel and financing the church.

HISTORY OF THE NEGRO CHURCH

Some of the faults as well as some of the strong points of these organizations stand out in bolder relief when the history of the transition from African tribal customs to American institutions is briefly traced. There have been four periods in the religious development of the Negro in the United States: (1) A period when masters feared to have slaves baptized because of the belief that it was illegal to hold Christians in slavery. (2) A short period when the evangelization of slaves was actively carried on and slaves met for worship in separate congregations or jointly with their masters. (3) A period when fear of slave revolts and uprisings made masters endeavor to check separate gatherings of slaves and consequently conduct joint services. (4) The period since the Civil War, when the Negro church has developed as a separate institution. During all of these stages the development of colored churches has been the result of the struggle of the Negro soul for religious self-expression, aided on the one hand by the missionary spirits of the white denominations, but often opposed by the fears and suspicions of those ruled by the economic motive.

For almost a hundred years (1619–1701) the religious instruction of Negro slaves was held in check by the unwritten law that a Christian could not be held as a slave. In permitting slaves to be introduced into the colonies, however, European sovereigns stipulated that such slaves should first have embraced Christianity, but there was little supervision of the slave trade and not much evidence that this provision was enforced against the opposition of the planters. English colonists were primarily interested in building homes in the New World and looked upon the Negro as a means to that end rather than as a human being in need of religious teaching. The scattering number of records of baptized Negroes indicates that a few of the more religious planters, even in this period, were scrupulous about the religious instruction of their slaves.

In Maryland, the only Catholic colony, the practice of preaching the gospel to white and colored alike began early. In the Protestant colonies, on the other hand, the formation, in 1701, of the Society for the Propagation of the Gospel in Foreign Parts, marked the beginning of systematic efforts to indoctrinate slaves. This was an English society which operated from 1701 up to the time of the

Revolutionary War and then withdrew. As late as 1667 Virginia passed the following law :

Baptism doth not alter the condition of the person as to his bondage or freedom, in order that diverse masters freed from doubt may more carefully endeavor the propagation of Christianity.

In 1670 Locke's Fundamental Constitutions of Carolina included the following article :

Since charity obliges us to wish well to the souls of all men, and religion ought to alter nothing in any man's civil estate or right, it shall be lawful for slaves as well as others to enter themselves and be of what church or profession any of them shall think best, and thereof be as fully members as any freeman. But yet no slave shall hereby be exempted from that civil dominion his master hath over him, but be in all things in the same state and condition he was in before.

In 1685, the French Code Noir made baptism and religious instruction of slaves obligatory. These laws and the agitation of Cotton Mather, John Eliot, Oglethorpe, Count Zinzendorf, and later (1766) of John Wesley, paved the way for a rather rapid evangelization of Negroes. The missionaries of the Society for the Propagation of the Gospel combed the South and reported many conversions of Negroes. In some places Negro congregations were formed and in others they met with the white people. The Moravians or United Brethren began early to establish separate missions for Negroes. Their influence was felt in Virginia, Carolina, and Georgia. Methodism was introduced in New York in 1766 and the first missionaries sent out by Wesley in 1769. From the very beginning they preached to both white and black and the denomination rapidly secured a colored membership. In 1800 they began to advocate the policy of appointing colored preachers for colored congregations, and Richard Allen, later founder of the African Methodist Episcopal Church, was the first appointed. The Baptists did not really get well started in the Southern states until about 1790, but at this time great revivals were held and many Negroes enrolled. It is reported that:

In general the Negroes were followers of the Baptists in Virginia, and after a while, as they permitted many colored men to preach, the great majority of them went to hear preachers of their own color, which was attended with many evils. — *Atlanta University Publication No. 8*, p. 18.

This policy was largely responsible for the rapid growth of the colored Baptist congregations, whose membership in 1793 was estimated to be one-fourth of the total membership in the denomination, or about 18,000. The same year the Methodists reported 16,227 colored members. Thus at the beginning of the nineteenth century the Methodists and Baptists had large colored memberships, each approaching twenty thousand. There was only a sprinkling of Presbyterians and Episcopalians.

At this time, however, forces of unrest began to work in the slave population. The same unrest which caused Toussaint L'Ouverture to lead the Haitians in revolt against their French masters spread to the United States and something of the spirit of liberty which flamed in the Colonial revolution found its way into Negro minds. Religious gatherings formed excellent places to talk these things over and they became marked as the centers of unrest. In 1800 South Carolina declared:

It shall not be lawful for any number of slaves, free Negroes, mulattoes, or mestizos, even in company with white persons, to meet together and assemble for the purpose of mental instruction or religious worship, either before the rising of the sun or after the going down of the same.

Later this was amended to allow a minority of Negroes to remain in meeting with white people. A similar act was passed in Virginia, but masters were allowed to employ religious teachers for their slaves.

The Denmark Vesey plot in Charleston in 1822 and the Nat Turner revolt in Virginia in 1831 illustrate, however, that these restrictions were not rigidly enforced and that agitators still found black congregations upon whose minds they could work. These plots and the economic revolution by which the cotton industry became so dominant led to a wave of restrictive legislation.

Virginia declared, in 1831, that neither slaves nor free Negroes might preach, nor could they attend religious services at night without permission. In North Carolina slaves and free Negroes were forbidden to preach, exhort, or teach. Maryland and Georgia had similar laws. The Mississippi law of 1831 said: "It is unlawful for any slave, free Negro, or mulatto to preach the gospel."   In Alabama the law of 1832 prohibited the assembling of more than five male slaves off the plantation to which they belonged, but the act was not to be considered as forbidding attendance at places of public worship held by white persons.

This left the religious worship of Negroes entirely to their masters. Many were included in white congregations and all the ante-bellum churches of the South have galleries in which the slaves sat. But only the favored few could obtain seats in these galleries and the masses of field hands were dependent upon the occasional visit of the itinerant preacher, or the family and plantation services held by devout masters and mistresses.

The Negro church membership increased from about 50,000 in 1800 to 468,000 in 1859. This increase of 900 per cent in sixty years indicated that, on the whole, the forces favoring the evangelization of Negroes were much stronger than the oppressive forces. In fact the oppression came more in waves impelled by fear and the forces of evangelization operated constantly.

Even before emancipation, friction in mixed congregations led to separate worship in many places. The colored people either used the same church edifice at different hours, or a separate edifice was erected for them. Nevertheless, they remained in the same church organization and some of the ablest white preachers of the time filled their pulpits and some of the ablest laymen taught their Sunday schools. Men of the type of Stonewall Jackson and Robert E. Lee held Sunday schools for colored people each Sunday and put their whole heart into this work of instruction.

Principal Denominations

The real tragedy of reconstruction was that these contacts were broken, and the colored church left to work out its own salvation in separate organizations. The African Methodist Episcopal Church was founded as a separate organization by Richard Allen even before the war, but its activities were almost entirely confined to the North.

After emancipation it spread south. From the galleries of the Southern Methodist Church the Colored Methodist Episcopal denomination grew. Later the African Methodist Episcopal Zion was added. Though in separate congregations the Baptists remained in the same conventions for some time, but the increasing pressure for self-determination on the part of the colored Baptists finally led to the organization of the National Baptist Convention. All the regular Baptist colored churches are now in separate denominational organizations.

The Baptist and the Methodist bodies include practically the whole colored population. Of the 4,600,000 church members 2,967,000 are in colored Baptist organizations and 54,000 are in colored congregations included in white Baptist organizations. Colored Methodist organizations embrace 1,068,000 and the Methodist Episcopal Church has enrolled 320,000 in separate colored congregations. The Protestant Episcopal Church has never divided into white and colored wings. Though its colored membership is small, the colored congregations belong to the same synods as the white congregations and some colored suffragan bishops are appointed by the church. Similarly, the Roman Catholic and the Presbyterian congregations, with the exception of some colored Cumberland Presbyterians, are included in the white organizations.

Although much valuable contact with the white race was lost by the organization of these separate colored denominations, this was in part compensated for by the fact that the Negro has gained in experience by having these great religious institutions as a training ground in organization and administration.

Emotional Services

There are to be found to-day among the city churches many orderly and well-administered congregations. Many of the country churches and some of the town congregations, on the other hand, have assumed many crudities.

A Negro investigator in a Northern city found three types of churches "whose services can be described by no better terms than religious hysteria." These are (1) congregations which are members of standard denominations, but which have wandered afield in their conduct of services; (2) special denominations, such as "Church of God" and "Saints of Christ"; and (3) congregations and organizations built up around individual preachers or leaders who split off from other churches. In these he found much hysteria. The services were characterized by singing, moaning, and shouting, shaking of the body, jumping, and rolling on the floor. This type of congregation is slowly giving ground before the advance of better trained preachers and the development of better self-control.

Factionalism

One of the handicaps which has seriously hampered the development of the colored church has been the tendency of congregations to split and form two weak churches where one was adequate. Factional rows are chiefly responsible for these splits. This has given the colored people the burden of too many organizations. In fact they are over-churched. The census of 1916 gives 39,655 Negro organizations. On the basis of the 1920 population this is a church for every 262 people. Their average membership was 116 as against 190 for the white churches. There are not nearly enough trained ministers to fill so many pulpits and those now in the pulpit are handicapped by the limited finances and uncertain support of such small congregations. The congregations, in turn, are handicapped by the poorer quality of preaching and inadequacy of the church edifices. Negro churches showed in 1916 a combined valuation of property amounting to $86,809,970, or an average value of $2189 per church. It is obvious that this sum will not adequately house a congregation.

There is some evidence, however, that this tendency to split has not operated so strongly in recent years as it did formerly. From 1906 to 1916 the membership in colored churches increased 24.7 per cent, but the number of organizations increased only 7.8 per cent. This would seem to indicate that the later tendency is toward the consolidation and strengthening of existing organizations rather than the formation of new ones. This tendency is one to be encouraged in every way possible, for the church has lost much ground through its divisions and dissensions.

RELATION TO THE COMMUNITY

The emotional character of the worship in some churches has been touched upon. The other outstanding characteristic of the colored church is the extent to which it is the center of the life of the people. At the close of the Civil War it was the one institution, and the minister was the one leader of the people. It therefore early became the agent not only for Sunday worship, but also for Bible classes, debating clubs, and social functions. The preacher was an adviser on temporal as well as spiritual matters.

Lodges sprang up from church congregations. Benefit societies and labor bureaus were among the activities fostered and, more recently, the church has entered the field of social welfare by adding institutional features.

No one is properly introduced to the colored community unless his introduction comes through the church and no movement can hope for wide success among the masses of the people which does not use the influence of the minister as its greatest asset. This has made even a more useful field for the colored institutional church than for similar white institutions. A few of the city churches have begun to develop along these lines. The Congregational Church of Atlanta numbers among its activities a working girls' home, an old folks' home, and numbers of young people's clubs. Big Bethel A.M.E. Church of the same city has for years operated a labor exchange and coöperated with the relief agencies of the city. The Atlanta Mutual Life Insurance Company grew from a benefit society formed in Wheat Street Baptist Church and this church engages its members in many other activities. In Jacksonville, Memphis, Richmond, and numbers of other cities, forward-looking ministers are developing institutions of real service and rooting their church deep in the life of their race.

This line of community service is one which should especially interest the country church. As yet, however, little progress toward institutional service has been made in rural districts. Churches have multiplied so fast that they have been unable to secure trained pastors, and have subdivided into such small congregations that they cannot afford to pay a man for full-time work. Consequently many preachers serve two, three, and four churches. This means that they are non-resident pastors, coming into the community on Saturday or Sunday morning and leaving Monday. They leave behind a group of untrained church officers who are unable to make the community activities of the church what they should be. Practically all the money collected in such churches goes to pay the preacher, and little remains for rendering service to the congregation. After surveying the rural church in Macon County, Alabama, where there are many absentee pastors, Rev. G. Lake Imes of Tuskegee concludes:

Little or no time is given to pastoral visitation. Scant attention is given to the school. No service is rendered in the week-day interests of the people, and this is the result: that while the people of this community contribute nearly four times as much to religion as they do to education, they receive in the time of the pastor, and the upkeep of the church, only one-sixth as much in return as they receive from the schools. In short, the church and the preacher are in grave danger of becoming mere parasites in the life of our people.

It is therefore evident that where there is a resident preacher the church is a most powerful institution in the colored community, but where denominational or factional splits have so overchurched a community that the small congregations cannot support resident pastors, much work is needed to harness the potential influence of the church on community life. The remedies lie in the consolidation and strengthening of present congregations to the point where more of the pastor's time can be demanded, in more frequent use of rural church buildings as social centers, in systematic efforts to give more training to the local church officials, — the deacons and elders, and in more interest in utilizing the church as a means of community uplift during the whole month rather than every other or every fourth Sunday.

SUNDAY SCHOOLS

One natural result of the interest of the church in temporal matters has been the adoption of an educational policy by practically every denomination. This educational policy embraces not only the Sunday school, but also contributions to the support of denominational schools.

Colored Sunday schools may be characterized by the statement that, as a rule, they are well attended, but, outside of the larger city churches, they are poorly organized. Too many ministers look upon their Sunday school as a useless adjunct which deflects attention from their regular service, instead of realizing in it a source of vital power from which the church can draw young members.

The features of the Sunday school which need strengthening are those of organization and administration. Better grading of the scholars, a clearer understanding by the teachers of their tasks, better equipment, and better administrative programs, are points where marked improvement could be made with a little intelligent effort and a small expenditure of funds.

As yet the large colored denominations, the African Methodist Episcopal, the African Methodist Episcopal Zion, and the Baptist, have not begun to approach this task systematically, and the Colored Methodist Episcopal Church has just made a small beginning. What is needed is field work, — visitation and instruction by trained workers who can go into the church community, discover the leaders, and arouse them to the task of reaching young people.

In some states the white Baptists with some financial aid from the colored Baptists have supported colored Sunday school organizers who, for a while, rendered valuable service. For the most part, however, these workers have been discontinued for the lack of funds. If the colored Baptists were fully alive to the magnitude of this need, they are fully able, without the aid of the white denomination, to support such workers with the proceeds of one annual Sunday school collection from each church.

The work of the Presbyterian Church in the U. S. A. is to be especially commended in this line. While this denomination embraces only about 30,000 colored members, they have 27 full-time Sunday school workers in the field whose mission is threefold. They go out and discover neglected communities in which there is no Sunday school and organize one. They visit homes and give the people Bibles and literature, and instruct them in family prayer. They visit schools already organized and help them with their problems of grading, teaching, and equipment. They maintain in Atlanta a well-organized publication bureau for the distribution of literature and information to these field workers, and once a year they hold four Sunday school institutes.

SECULAR EDUCATION

Many adult Negroes in the early days first learned to read in the Sunday school. It was but a short step from this kind of Sunday school to a parochial school, where the simple elementary subjects were taught by the preacher or by a hired teacher. The consolidation of these parochial schools has given each denomination something of a system of education.

The African Methodist Episcopal Church supports a school in each Southern state and, in Morris Brown University, this denomination has a college of increasing size and rising standards. In coöperation with the Southern Methodist (white) the Colored Methodist Episcopal Church has 9 schools. The Methodist Episcopal Church, which includes the white Methodists in the North and quite a large colored membership in the South, has 18 large schools. The Presbyterian denomination (Presbyterian Church in the U. S. A.) maintains 85 schools, most of which are small, but several of which are important. The Protestant Episcopal Church, which is also one of mixed membership, maintains 10 large and 14 small schools. The Congregational board supports 29 schools, all of which are important.

The Baptists have suffered greatly through the decentralization of their educational work. In other words, their parochial schools have not consolidated to any great extent beyond the local association. These associations embrace only a few counties each and are not financially able to support a large school. This has given the colored Baptists 110 schools, only 31 of which could be classed as of any importance other than that of supplementing the local public schools. In coöperation with the American Baptist Home Mission Society (white), however, the Colored Baptists contribute to 24 large schools, some of which are among the most important in the country for training colored leaders.

The combined incomes of the schools of denominations with all colored membership was, in 1916, $381,000, while the combined income of the schools supported by denominations of mixed white and colored membership was

$1,550,000. Thus the church is making a real and increasingly important contribution to the training of colored leadership.

MORALITY AND THRIFT

While the church has been of great service to the race in reaching large numbers with an evangelical message and in serving the people as a many-functioned institution, it has not fully measured up to its opportunities of inculcating greater thrift and morality in its members. This should be interpreted, not so much as a detraction from the great part which the church has played in building Negro character as a challenge to go ahead with a task well begun. Were it not for the colored church, Negro home and family life would be nowhere near as moral as it is to-day, yet there is much room for improvement.

One of the greatest gaps which had to be bridged between Africa and America was in the life of the home and the family. The African system was one of polygamous clans. The slave was uprooted from an existence ordered under this plan and placed upon a plantation where monogamy was theoretically demanded but in many cases not really expected. This, according to the Atlanta University Study of the Negro Church, practically amounted to a new polygamy with all of the evils and none of the benefits of the African system.

The African system was a complete protection for girls, and a strong protection for wives against everything but the tyranny of the husband; the plantation polygamy left the chastity of Negro women absolutely unprotected in law, and practically little guarded in custom. The number of wives of a West Indian slave was limited chiefly by his lust and cunning. The black females, were they wives or growing girls, were the legitimate prey of the men, and on this system there was one and only one safeguard, the character of the master of the plantation.

Since emancipation, the white man's law and the black man's church have been the only safeguards of family morality and of the two the church has been more potent than the law. It has not, however, measured up to this responsibility as fully as it could have if the ministers had addressed themselves whole-heartedly to this task from the beginning, and had their services contained less of evangelical fire and theological dogma and more lessons of thrift and morality. In other words, there is a great need, which is slowly being met, that the Negro church be more intimately related to the lives of its individual members in its preaching as it is in its institutional features.

As in the white population, this tendency to overemphasize evangelism and the resultant failure to relate the teachings of the pulpit intimately to life has begun to estrange the younger generation from the church. They do not attend as regularly as their parents. Should this tendency operate unchecked for several generations the colored church would be in danger of losing its preëminent place in the life of the race.

PREACHERS

The multiple activities of colored ministers call for a training above the average and yet the training facilities are wholly inadequate to meet this great demand. As has been noted there are almost 40,000 Negro churches and only about 19,000 ministers. This means that fully 25,000

Negro churches are without the services of a full-time minister, and have services only twice a month or once a month, according to the number of other pulpits filled by their minister. The numerical problem of securing a sufficient force to supply these half-filled pulpits is, in itself, a great one. At the time of the Bureau of Education Survey of Negro Schools (1916) the combined output of all colored theological schools did not aggregate 200 per year. It is not at all uncommon to find pulpits filled by men who during the week are teachers or tradesmen. But until the weaker colored churches are better organized and more securely financed, there is not much need for a greater number of preachers, because, if they were available these weaker congregations could not now support a full-time pastor. The problem is rather one of increasing the training and efficiency of the ministers now in the pulpit with the assurance of a fairly steady and adequate annual crop of young men to enter the profession.

From county studies we may picture the average rural colored preacher thus : He is a man who can read and write, usually a man of considerable native intelligence and oratorical ability, but a man with meager elementary education (only about 1 per cent have had any theological training and from 3 to 5 per cent have had high school training). He is handicapped by small, shifting, and poorly organized congregations. For his labors he receives from $150 to $500 per year and consequently has to supplement this by farming or operating a small business. In fully 90 per cent of the cases he serves more than one church. This means that he stands in the relation of non-resident pastor to at least one of his congregations and sees them only on the day when he preaches, leaving them without ministerial services for the rest of the month or two weeks between his sermons.

One of the criticisms frequently lodged against colored ministers and congregations is that the financial management of the smaller churches is lax. This condition arises partly from the failure of the untrained minister to keep adequate accounts and provide for annual audits, and partly from the failure of the congregations themselves through their officers, to pay their assessments promptly and fulfill their obligations in business-like manner. Many colored preachers have to waste much time and energy at the end of each year in holding "rallies" to collect salary which should have been paid them regularly through the year.

CHURCH COÖPERATION

In planning these details of church management the white ministers and church officers could render valuable advisory service if they were called in to discuss problems with the colored minister. In the past much more of this friendly advice was given than now, but there are still many white men who would be pleased to render such service if asked to do so.

The controversies over slavery and the bitterness of the Civil War estranged white from colored congregations, and separated Northern from Southern congregations within three great denominations. Opinion was divided to such a point that organized Christianity in the United States has no unified policy toward the colored race even though the love of Christ for all races, nations, and classes of mankind, is woven all through the New Testament.

The doctrine, "Go ye into all the world," has been interpreted by Southern denominations as a command to go into foreign fields, and they have spent many millions of dollars for foreign missions as against very small amounts for the great home mission work among the Negroes at their door. In the words of a Southern man, W. D. Weatherford:

Here at our very door is one of the greatest and most fertile mission fields the world knows. . . . What princely givers we have been! The Presbyterians last year gave an average of three postage stamps per member to this work. The Methodists averaged less than the price of a cheap soda water — just a five cent one. The Southern Baptist Convention has only been asking from its large membership $15,000 annually, or less than one cent per member for this tremendous work.

The general boards of white denominations can render great service to the colored church along several lines. One of the most important is assistance in strengthening the facilities for training colored ministers. Each colored denomination should be aided by its affiliated white denomination to develop its preacher-training facilities. There is also a big opportunity to train preachers now on the job through summer institutes. The Southern Methodist Episcopal Church conducts several of these institutes for Colored Methodist Episcopal pastors and the results have been excellent. Such institutes are held in connection with several schools, but this movement is so recent that very few of the active ministers have yet been reached.

The second great field of service of the white boards to the colored boards is in assistance with the Sunday school program. Some description has been given of the aid extended by the Presbyterian Church in the U. S. A. through field Sunday school organizers. A little financial assistance and some coöperation in working out literature and institute plans would prove a great stimulus to the colored church boards in extending their Sunday school work.

In local communities many mutual problems could be profitably discussed in joint ministers' meetings. The plan of organizing white and colored ministerial unions which meet separately three times and jointly once a month is gaining in favor. The Atlanta Christian Council is modeled on this plan and many useful coöperative projects have been fathered by this body and mutual aid on these projects has, in turn, contributed to a better feeling between the races.

Local churches also have a fine opportunity for home mission activity in developing colored mission Sunday schools in neglected settlements. A pioneer in this line was the Rev. John Little of Louisville, Ky., whose Sunday school is supported and taught by members of a large white Presbyterian congregation. This work has expanded until the school is now active all week. The Bible is taught on Sundays, and industries on week days. The effect of this industrial training and of neighborhood clubs centering in the school has made its influence felt throughout one of the neediest sections of the city.

The Federal Council of Churches has taken a significant step in the formation of a commission on race relations composed of churchmen of both races and many denominations. This commission is beginning to coördinate the interracial activities among the churches and promote constructive local coöperation especially among the Federated

Church Councils in Northern cities. They have rendered valuable service in the campaign against lynching; they have promoted the observance of race relations Sunday; they maintain a useful information service and are stimulating study projects.

It would be difficult to conceive of a more fruitful field for the application of practical Christian principles, for translating the social treachings of Jesus into actual life, than the field of race relations. The young church members of each race need to realize this thoroughly and build the church organizations of the future generation on the basis of mutual helpfulness and unity of spirit.

BIBLIOGRAPHY

Atlanta University Publications No. 8.
BRAWLEY, BENJAMIN. A Short History of the American Negro, Chapter XI.
HAYNES, G. E. The Trend of the Races.
The Atlanta Plan of Interracial Coöperation.
United States Census — Religious Bodies, 1916.
WEATHERFORD, W. D. Present Forces in Negro Progress, Chapter VI.
WOODSON, CARTER G. History of the Negro Church, pp. 286–296.

TOPICS FOR STUDY AND DISCUSSION

1. Discuss the Negro Church as the center of Negro social life.

2. What has been the training of the Negro preachers of your community?

3. What efforts do white denominations in your state make to aid Negro denominations or congregations: (1) in training preachers; (2) in Sunday school organization and supervision; (3) in evangelical activities; (4) in social service?

4. What local organizations promote coöperation between white and colored churches?

5. How many Negro churches in your community are the result of splits in one congregation? Get in touch with the leaders in such a church and get the facts behind the split. Study these facts and see if they indicate any significant conclusion. What effect has the split had on church finances and leadership?

6. Is there any relation between illiteracy and the emotional type of church service?

7. How do you account for the fact that Baptists and Methodists are so predominant among the Negroes?

CHAPTER XII

RACE CONTACTS

A consideration of the elements of race adjustment outlined in the preceding chapters will reveal that where the races come together for educational effort, for health improvement, for moral advance, or for humanitarian ends, the community as a whole benefits and the mutual respect of the two races increases. It is impossible to work consistently with a man and hate him. On the other hand, the contacts of the vicious and criminal element, contacts which lead to amalgamation of races, or those that are even symbols of social intermixture, contacts of violence and exploitative economic contacts, make for race antagonism. In other words, both the relationships which make for progress and those which make for friction may be expressed in terms of contacts. Contacts may therefore be classified as follows: Helpful — health improvement, educational effort, moral advance, safeguarding law, religious, civic improvement, humanitarian effort, economic coöperation; Harmful — vice and crime, social intermingling, violence, economic exploitation and unfair competition, and demagogic or exploitative political contacts.

If the races are to live at peace and make progress in the United States, the simplest formula which can be given to them is that the helpful contacts should be increased and strengthened by every possible device, and that each individual of both races seek the means of cultivating these contacts; that the harmful contacts be safeguarded and discontinued wherever possible, and that individuals of each race set their faces against such contacts.

A fine recent utterance of this principle was voiced in the inaugural address of Governor Whitfield of Mississippi:

Wise leaders among the Negroes must be encouraged in their splendid efforts to aid their own people. Points of agreement between the races must be emphasized and points of friction minimized. Every man and woman in the state must see to it that the laws protecting the Negroes in their lives and property are rigorously enforced; that the occasional white man who seeks to profit through the ignorance of his tenants or laborers be forced by the overwhelming weight of an aroused public opinion to give a square deal to all whom he employs, regardless of race or color, and that there be the fullest coöperation between the white man and the black, to the end that peace and prosperity come to the white and black alike through cordial coöperation in the agricultural and industrial upbuilding of the state.

Segregation

Where the races have lived side by side for some time, each type of contact has created a code of meeting, — a contact behavior which has become customary and understood by both races. As is usual with customs and folkways, these codes are often difficult to rationalize. For instance, even where "Jim Crow" laws are most stringent against the mixing of the races in railway coaches, it is not at all unusual to see a colored nurse riding with a white mother and child. In fact such a situation is specifically exempted from most of the separate coach statutes. It is understood. The explanation is that the nurse's presence is in no way a symbol of social intermingling. Again, the two races in the South are to be found working side by side on the same building as carpenters or masons. Here also the relationship is well understood. The men coöperate in work, laugh and joke amicably together, but it is perfectly understood that neither will invite the other home to dinner or extend their personal relationships beyond a certain indefinable line. An interesting illustration of this economic relationship is shown in the story of the Englishman who ran out of money in South Africa and consented to work for a native contractor on condition that the native call him "boss."

The unanalytical are inclined to dismiss such behavior phenomena as the result of illogical prejudice, but illogical though they may be, they arise from roots far deeper than prejudice. Primarily they may be explained by the fundamental sociological principle of consciousness of kind, of pleasurable association with similars. The "we-group" always sets up protective taboos and restrictions against intermarriage and to some extent against intermingling with the "other-than-we-group," especially if there is a wide ethnic difference between the two.

When the undesirability of racial amalgamation is admitted, either from a biological or a social standpoint, then the necessity for certain forms of separation which tend to miminize social contacts is apparent. They are the results of the effort to create a code under which it is possible to be "brothers in Christ without becoming brothers-in-law."

A second tendency toward the separation of racial activities results from the tendency to specialization. Whenever an organization is designed to serve the Negro's special needs or develop his special capabilities, there is a tendency for a separate colored organization or a colored branch of an existing organization to be formed. The most notable example of the specialization of service is seen in the voluntary formation of large Negro congregations within white denominations and the formation of large separate colored denominations. The peculiarly religious nature of the Negro and his desire for a special type of worship and of religious leadership has exerted a pressure which has led him to specialize his own religious activity. It was also noted in an earlier chapter that Negro unionists often prefer a separate local union, which can not only specialize on their particular problems, but also coöperate with the white organization in district councils. The increasing number of colored doctors and their special need for hospital training is exerting a pressure for the development of separate colored hospitals. These types of specialization are obviously very different social phenomena from the arbitrary separation along social lines, and the two should not be confused.

There are forms of segregation which are cruel and others which are useless. Too often the separation of the Negro simply affords an opportunity to give him inadequate accommodations for the same pay, and does not help in preserving race purity. The majority of Negroes oppose separate railway coaches not because of an inherent desire to ride with white people, but because most railroads herd them into half coaches which are part colored passenger coach and part baggage car. Often there is only one toilet for both sexes, and sometimes the conductor, brakeman, or "news butcher," makes his headquarters in the colored compartment, forcing colored passengers to stand. Sometimes they are furnished wooden coaches which are dangerously sandwiched between the heavy steel coaches. Likewise the Negro does not move out into a white residence neighborhood because of the desire to live with white people, but because of the desire to escape the noxious surroundings commonly found in Negro settlements — lack of police protection, dismal lighting, filthy streets, and cramped quarters. In other words, all that most Negroes see in separation is that it is a means to degrade and an opportunity to exploit them. So long as it presents this aspect to them, it will be galling and insulting, and they will oppose it. Stated positively, this means that in the final analysis if segregation is to be successfully maintained, it must not be confused with discrimination and must finally be approved by the colored people themselves as beneficial to race relations.

The administration of segregation regulations by minor functionaries, who are often prejudiced and brutal toward the weaker race, is an additional source of irritation to the Negro. It has been the author's observation that the attitude of colored people toward separation in street cars in certain towns has been radically altered by efforts of the company to secure uniform courtesy and consideration on the part of its conductors. In the hands of ignorant and prejudiced employees segregation can be made a smarting insult.

There was one railroad station from which colored people were permitted to embark by one gate but into which they were compelled to return by another gate. In the absence of any sign directing them there was constant confusion. Of course a man could not be supposed to know by instinct that he was permitted to depart along with white people through a certain gate but not to come back with them through the same gate. To make matters worse the gate-keepers were uniformly gruff and domineering and the resultant effect of this arrangement was to embitter the whole colored populace of the surrounding territory. One day the gate-keeper roughly seized a man who was innocently trying to depart through the same gate through which he entered. When the man in his surprise jerked violently away, only the quick action of some cool heads prevented a near riot. In their own councils Negroes discuss and often magnify these things until they loom large in their race consciousness. As Dr. R. R. Moton expresses it, such petty, nagging restrictions are "gravels in the Negro's shoe, small in size but capable of inflicting great discomfort and impeding progress."

Apart from manifest inequalities in separate accommodations and insulting methods of applying segregation, many colored citizens seem happier in their own company than when the company is mixed. There is also evidence that a growing race pride is strengthening the feeling of colored people against racial intermixture. But if the white South is ever to justify segregation and maintain it on any democratic basis, it will be through the provision of accommodations which are as nearly equal as possible and through an administration which is just and considerate.

However, unless those forms of separation which are meant to safeguard the purity of the races are present, the majority of the white people flatly refuse to coöperate with Negroes. In other words, the preservation of racial integrity seems to be a fixed policy of the white people, and is becoming a fixed policy of the colored people. The solution of this situation would seem to rest in the imposition only of such forms of segregation as aid in the preservation of racial integrity, and in the administration of the system with absolute justice. If, in the long run, the wisdom and justice of such a system is not recognized by the Negro himself, there will either be constant discontent and friction or amalgamation. There is no alternative to these two, except the systematic minimization of social contacts.

PUBLIC OPINION AND THE PRESS

Any treatment of racial contacts would be incomplete without consideration of the indirect contacts which come from reading about or talking about each other, and which are generally referred to as public opinion. Public opinion is often different from the realities of a situation, and especially is this true of public opinion concerning race relations. It rests in part upon traditional belief and to this extent does not allow for change and progress. Current public opinion is formed largely by the press and the pulpit, and when these sources are poisoned by fear, by demagoguery, or by propaganda, the opinion which they form is wide of the facts.

An analysis of the comments on the Negro question in white dailies and periodicals reveals an undue emphasis upon crime and upon the ridiculous elements, with too little of constructive news and editorial policy. The Chicago Race Commission listed 1338 Negro news items which appeared over a period of two years in three principal white Chicago dailies. Of these 667, or one half, were concerned with riots, clashes, crime, vice, and illegitimate contacts; 551 were concerned with such impersonal matters as soldiers, politics, housing, sports, and migration; while only 58 were on such constructive subjects as education, art, business, and miscellaneous meetings.

The same investigation indicted the press North and South as the purveyor of an "inordinately one-sided picture." In the sensational headlining of race matters, the difference between North and South is only one of degree. In support of this the Chicago report quotes the following headlines:

NEGRO ROBBER ATTACKS WOMAN NEAR HER HOME

POLICE HUNT FOR NEGRO WHO HELD UP WOMAN

AUSTIN WOMAN ATTACKED IN HER OWN HOME BY NEGRO

WOMAN SHOCKED BY NEGRO THIEF

NEGRO ATTACKS WOMAN

ARREST NEGRO SUSPECT FIND MUCH IN POCKETS, etc.

It will be observed that the word "Negro" is prominently displayed in each case. This, according to colored leaders, is no more justified than would be the prominent display of "red headed" in every case where such an individual committed a crime. Such a policy foments race hatred and constantly holds in front of the white world the worst side of the Negro community, without any counterbalancing view of the better side. The constant impact of these sensational headings upon the public mind can hardly be estimated. It is a fact that nearly every race riot has been preceded by an orgy of newspaper sensationalism of the most inflammatory type.

Ray Stannard Baker, in his investigations of the Atlanta riot, noted the effect of the glaring, sensational headlines displayed several days before this outbreak and pointed out that some of these sensations later evaporated as mere rumors. East St. Louis was prepared for her bloody riot by a similar sensational deluge of the public mind. General Wood in taking charge after the Omaha riot stated that the responsibility for the strained relations there rested upon a few individuals and one newspaper. The Chicago report gives the following succinct account of the sensation which paved the way for the Washington riot: "The Washington race riot was precipitated by reports of alleged attacks upon white women by Negroes. These reports were featured in the daily newspapers with large front-page headlines, and suggestions were made that probable lynchings would follow the capture of the Negroes. The series of reported assaults totaled seven. In each it was claimed that a Negro had assaulted a white woman. When the fury and excitement of the riot had subsided and the facts were sifted, it was found that of the seven assaults reported, four were assaults upon colored women. Three of the alleged criminals arrested and held for assault were white men, and at least two of the white men were prosecuted for assaults upon colored women. It further developed that three of the assaults were supposed to have been committed by a suspect who at the time of the riots was under arrest."

Although the colored press rants against the white press for its unbalanced news and editorial policy, it is, in its way, fully as one-sided and as potent in its contribution to racial antagonism. According to the Chicago Commission's study of the three Chicago colored papers: "The news items in

Negro papers show a bias in reporting the opposite of that of many white papers. They emphasize the Negro view, frequently to the point of distorting fact. If anything, they might be said to provide a compensatory interpretation of the news."

The painstaking study of Prof. Robert T. Kerlin of Virginia Military Institute, published under the title "The Voice of the Negro," contains ample evidence that the Negro papers give too much space to the sensational treatment of discrimination, grievances, rights, riots, lynchings. Professor Kerlin holds that no one can know the mind of the Negro without studying their journals, "The Negro has discovered the power and importance of his own press. It is a rapidly expanding influence, consisting even now of two dailies, a dozen magazines, and over three hundred weeklies. In it may be found the voice of the Negro and his heart and mind."

The situation is discouraging to any one interested in peace and good will between the races. On one side the white press assails the white mind with constant impact from the worst phases of Negro life; on the other side the Negro press assails the Negro mind with constant impact from the worst side of white life. Between the two they have fomented much discontent and several riots, and if their policy remains unchanged, they will inevitably stir up much more discontent and many more riots. The press of both races has seemed only too well contented to sacrifice the chances for racial peace and progress in order to build a profitable circulation by catering to the widespread pleasure derived from the sensational story.

It must be said, however, that much of the damage done to race relations by this policy has been unintentional. Very

recently white editors have shown a tendency to come together and face this issue, and have manifested a willingness
to change their policies when they have fully realized their
import. More than fifty editors representing six Southern
states recently declared; "It would be well if even greater
effort was made to publish news of a character which is
creditable to the Negro, showing his development as a
people along desirable lines. This would stimulate him to
try to attain a higher standard of living." Such a policy is
well worthy of the consideration of all press associations.
Similarly, more effort is being made to get constructive news
into the Negro papers, not as an effort to suppress the facts
concerning real grievances and outrages, but in order to
complete the picture by showing both sides of the question.

CONCLUSION

It must always be remembered that the relations between
white and black are but a part of the race problem in the
United States. Many students in Texas feel that their
Mexican problems are more complicated than their Negro
problems, and the people of the Pacific coast would not
qualify their statement that the questions raised by the
presence of Orientals are, to them, ten to one more important than Negro questions. In other sections, where people
of different nationalities of the white race are in contact,
they have their difficulties. The Negro is only one element
— the largest single element in the " melting pot."

Again it will be helpful for the student to remember that
the tasks of race relations in the United States are but a
part of the larger tasks throughout the world. In India
and Africa, England faces the black and the brown races.

Belgium and France also have their African tasks, while the Orient is a meeting ground for the white and the yellow, and the Near East is a hodgepodge of colors and stocks. Some of the successful principles of racial adjustment between the white and the Negro in the United States may apply to race relations in other areas and between other peoples. Certainly the fundamental principles of justice and of helpful coöperation are universal in their application.

The diffusion of Negroes throughout the United States has resulted in a spread and nationalization of racial contacts. Up to the time of the recent migrations, contacts were largely localized in the South and the white people of other sections were in the position of bystanders — outsiders whose comments were often resented. Now, however, the whole nation is vitally concerned with the satisfactory adjustment of race relations and is showing a desire to face these tasks in a truly American manner.

Race relations have become more national and less sectional because, in its expansion, the federal government has come into contact with the Negro in new ways. The use of Negro troops, aid to the Negro farmer, application of the various federal funds appropriated for education and public health, relation of the Negro to the labor problems of the nation, and the influence of the presence of large numbers of Negroes on the immigration policy are all concrete instances of the growth, altogether apart from party politics, of a national attitude, to replace the old sectional view of race contacts.

A review of the diverse tasks of adjusting race relations which have been outlined in the preceding chapters brings into bold relief the fact that no one panacea can be applied

as a cure-all. No one symptom can be isolated and called
"The Race Problem." Problems of race cross-section the
problems of democracy. In communities where the population is biracial, all community life is complicated by the
presence of the two races. There are many everyday tasks
of coöperation. This reflects back to the idea with which
the introduction of this book is concerned ; namely, that the
adjustment of race relations constitutes far more of a task
than a problem. There is a substantial' agreement as to
what needs to be done for leadership, for health, for education, for law and order, for economic advance, for religious
improvement, for social welfare. The performance of
these tasks demands the wisdom, fairness, and diplomacy of
the thoughtful members of both races. They are above the
realm of partisan politics and of sectionalism. They involve
the prosperity of communities, but even to a greater degree
they control the health and happiness of millions of individuals. They are human tasks and above all their humanitarian aspects should be emphasized. But the tasks that
remain involve methods of enabling the organizations now
dealing with these social problems to function for Negroes
as well as for white people.

Human personalities need to be recognized as the para-
mount issue. Antipathies and jealousies based upon the
opinion which one race holds of the other *en masse* need to
be submerged in the resolve to recognize individual merit
and individual worth. Thus the keynote of the approach to
racial adjustment is not that of partisanship, of sectionalism, or of self, but that of service, the type of service which
is consecrated to the benefit of the maximum number of
men, women, and children in the community.

BIBLIOGRAPHY

DuBois, W. E. B. Darkwater.
Detweiler, D. T. The Negro Press.
Kerlin, R. T. The Voice of the Negro.
The Negro in Chicago, Chapters VI and IX.

TOPICS FOR STUDY AND DISCUSSION

1. Pick some one form of race contact and study the number of individuals brought together and the frequency with which they are brought together. Study the customs surrounding this contact and endeavor to explain them. Does this contact make for race friction or for racial adjustment?

2. Study the places in your community where the races are separated by law or by custom. What are the reasons for separation in each case? Is the separation humanely or brutally enforced?

3. Study a separate Negro residence district. What effect has this separation on streets, police protection, lights, sanitation? What effect have these things on the Negro's attitude toward segregation?

4. Assuming that racial amalgamation is undesirable, is some form of separation necessary? How much?

5. Analyze the news and editorials in eight or ten issues of a Negro paper and determine the relative space given to different types of matter. What is the general effect of this paper on the Negro mind?

6. What contribution has the United States to make toward African colonial policies?

7. What has our domestic Negro problem to do with our international relations with South American countries, Mexico, the West Indies, Japan?

APPENDIX

SUGGESTIONS TO TEACHERS

"The Basis of Racial Adjustment" is a treatment of the significant aspects of the relations of the White and Negro races in the United States. For those who would use it as a text, bibliographies and discussion topics have been placed at the end of each chapter.

The teacher should study the topics and have on hand such material as census reports, reports of funds, and state departments and such other documents as can be turned over to the student for preparation of discussions. The minimum should be The Negro Year Book published by Tuskegee, Negro Population in the United States, 1790–1915 (Census Bureau), and such official reports as will be needed for reference by students assigned discussion topics.

If black and white people are to live peaceably and justly, they must learn to think in terms of the facts of race relations. The teacher's task is therefore not so much that of getting students to follow the printed pages of this book as it is to get them to think on the topics covered. For this reason the topics have been arranged so as to call for the maximum amount of first-hand observation. An hour of such observation, when it is properly directed, is worth ten hours of book study. Students are brought face to face with the realities in such a way that their own minds work out conclusions rather than accepting ready-made dogmas. They discover the facts in a concrete situation from which there is no appeal. Their interest is vitalized by the study of a real living situation rather than of a printed page. It is urged, therefore, that wherever possible teachers use this book merely as a basis for guiding first-hand observation of the community. Such a procedure will not only quicken the learning process but will yield the most fruitful results in translating this learning into the practical application of morality and democracy to interracial affairs.

To get the best results from this kind of study, topics for discussion should be assigned as far in advance as possible. It might be well to select all these topics and assign them to members of the class at its first meeting, so that they can begin immediately to read and observe. In the event interracial action is contemplated it might be well at this first meeting to designate an interracial committee to get in touch with Negro leaders and with other organizations in the community which are interested in constructive work.

The author is aware that many groups will have too short a time to devote a session to each chapter. For this reason the teacher is requested to study the interrelation of chapters so that they may be grouped logically. While the following plan provides only for superficial study it suggests a method of covering the book in eight sessions:

Session I. Organization and assignment. Study Chapters I and II.

Session II. (Chapters. III and IV.) The chapters on Population and Health are related and involve the factors of birth, death, health, and movement.

Session III. Chapters V and VI relate to the two aspects of the Negro's economic life and can be discussed together.

Session IV. Chapter VII is a most important chapter and if possible should be treated alone but could be combined with Chapter VIII, making a unit of law and government.

Session V. Devote to Chapter VIII, if VIII and VII are not combined.

Session VI. Education (Chapter IX) should by all means stand alone.

Session VII. Chapters X and XI naturally combine as they relate to the spiritual and humanitarian sides of the problem.

Session VIII. Chapter XII gives a good opportunity to review.

INDEX

African Methodist Episcopal Church,
  beginnings, 216, 218; schools, 226
African Methodist Episcopal Zion,
  219
Agitation and leadership, 22–28
Agriculture, 75–95; education for,
  189–193. *See* Farm
Alabama, percentage of Negroes in,
  41–42; emigration from, 52; anti-
  lynching laws, 144; property in,
  152, 153; school funds, 178; early
  religious laws, 217
Allen, Richard, 216, 218
Almshouses, 156, 201
Amalgamation, 3, 42–44, 237
American Federation of Labor, 51
Arkansas, percentage of Negroes in,
  41, 42; property in, 152, 153;
  school funds, 178
Arrests. *See* Crime
Asylums. *See* Insanity *and* Orphans
Atlanta, Georgia, 34; community
  chest, 209; Christian Council in,
  232; riot in, 243
Attucks, Crispus, 156, 158
Augusta, Georgia, 34

Baker, Ray Stannard, 243
Banks, 120, 121, 122
Banneker, Benjamin, 13
Baptists: Southern Baptist Conven-
  tion, 143; beginnings, 216, 219;
  schools, 226
Barbers, 119
Beggars, 199
Biology of race, 7–9
Birth rate, 40–41, 53
Black Belt, 41–42, 54, 179
Bond issues, 4
Brain weight, 172

Building trades. *See* Labor, skilled
Bunker Hill, battle of, 156, 158
Business, 119–123; retail, 120
Business League, 123, 193
Business men, 14, 21, 25
Butler, General B. F., 159

Calhoun, John, 170
Carnegie Foundation, 135
Carney, standard-bearer, 157
Carolina, Locke's Fundamental Con-
  stitutions, 215
Carver, George W., 13, 28
Charities, 200–202
Charleston, South Carolina, 217
Chattanooga, Tennessee, 34
Chicago Commission on Race Rela-
  tions, 102, 106, 241–243
Chicago, Illinois: School of Philan-
  thropy, 207; press, 241
Childbirth, 59–60
Child-placing. *See* Orphans
Children of servants, 101. *See*
  Schools, Infant mortality, Juve-
  nile delinquency
Christian Index, 142
Christianity, 212–233
Church, power of, 212; members,
  212; history, 213–218; opposi-
  tion to, 213–218; denominations,
  218–219; emotionalism, 220; fac-
  tionalism, 220; community centers, 221–224; institutional features, 222; officials, 223; Sunday
  schools, 224; morality of members, 227–228; preachers, 228–
  230; coöperation in, 230–233;
  segregation in, 237–238
Church of God, 220
Citizens, 149–152

253

Roman Catholic, 219
Rosenwald, Julius, 73, 187
Rosenwald Fund, 50, 170, 187
Rural institutions, 46, 62
Rural population, 41

Salem, Peter, 156
Sanitary inspection, 70
Savannah, Georgia, 34; battle of, 158
Schools, medical, 30; normal, 30;
theological, 30; private, 193–198,
225–227; professional, 195; for
social workers, 207. *See* Schools,
public
Schools, public: development, 21,
176; improvement, 50, 169, 177–
179,185–188; appropriations,155;
comparative expenditures, 177–
179; buildings, 180; term, 180–
181; attendance, 181; teachers,
181; county training, 182; high
schools,182–183; supervision,183,
185
Segregation, 236
Selfishness of leaders, 29–30
Sex ratio, 53
Slater Fund, 170, 186
Slave trade, 35, 214
Slavery, 7, 20, 35, 99
Smith-Hughes Act, 190
Social equality, 26–27
Social work, 207. *See* Probation *and*
Family case work
Society for the Propagation of the
Gospel, 215
Soldiers. *See* Patriots
South Carolina: interracial com-
mittee, 33; percentage of Negroes,
41–42; emigration, 52; health de-
partment, 67; anti-lynching laws,
144; property, 152–153; school
funds, 178; early religious laws,
217; slave revolt, 217
Special abilities, 5, 12, 13
Standard of living, 107
Standards of leaders, 30
State: departments of health, 66; su-
pervisors of schools, 185; schools,
188–191. *See individual states*
Strikes, 113

Sunday school, 224
Superiority, 11, 12

Talladega College, 69, 194
Tanner, H. O., 12
Taxation, 4, 152–156
Teachers, 14, 21, 25
Tenancy, extent, 77; evils, 79–80;
share, 80, 82; profits, 82–83; in-
crease, 84; contracts, 87–90; in
England, 89
Tennessee: interracial committee,
33–34; percentage of Negroes, 41;
emigration, 52; anti-lynching
laws, 145; property, 153; vot-
ing, 163; school funds, 178
Testimony, unreliability of, 136
Texas: percentage of Negroes in,
41–42; property in, 153; school
funds, 178
Theological schools, 30
Toussaint L'Ouverture. *See* L'Ou-
verture, Toussaint
Trades. *See* Labor
Tradition, 212, 213, 227
Tuberculosis: death rate, 53, 59–
60, 61–62; National Tuberculosis
Association, 65; state nurse, 67;
sanitaria, 67
Turner, Nat, 217
Tuskegee Institute, 21, 69, 107, 191–
193

Uncle Remus, 12
Unions. *See* Labor
United Brethren, 215
United States. *See* National govern-
ment
Urban League, National, 118
Urbanization. *See* City

Venereal disease, 41, 61
Vesey, Denmark, 217
Violence, 49–50
Virginia, percentage of Negroes in,
41–42; emigration from, 52; property in, 152–153; voting in, 163;
school funds, 178; religious laws,
215, 217; slave revolt, 217
Voting, 26, 150–151, 162–167